Friends of the Bridegroom

Marc Cardinal Ouellet

Friends of the Bridegroom

For a Renewed Vision of Priestly Celibacy

Translated by Benjamin Crockett

EWTN PUBLISHING, INC.
Irondale, Alabama

EWTN Publishing, Inc.
5817 Old Leeds Road, Irondale, AL 35210

Distributed by Sophia Institute Press, Box 5284, Manchester, NH 03108.

ISBN 978-1-68278-135-7

Library of Congress Control Number:2019949758

First printing

"What I came to do at Carmel,
I said at the feet of Jesus Christ,
In the exam that preceded my profession:
I have come to save souls
And especially in order to pray for priests."

—Saint Thérèse of the Child Jesus

Contents

Part 3

For a Priestly Spirituality
in the School of Saints

Friends of the Bridegroom

Introduction

Friends of the Bridegroom

Priests and bishops today live in a time of trial and even crisis, but with the grace of God and the will to respond to His Word this difficult time can become an opportunity for conversion and growth. If there was a time when the clergy reigned supreme over the flock of the faithful, at the risk of falling into clericalism, caste privilege, and abuse of power, that time is over. The scandals, humiliations, and wear and tear of recent years have plunged the upper and lower clergy into a state of vulnerability, if not distress, which can be recognized as signs of fatigue, tension, and even discouragement, to the point of reckless action.

Bishops are overwhelmed by the management of suspected or proven cases of abuse, and not just sexual abuse.[1] The results of surveys over the past decades, widely publicized, have caused concern, distress, almost panic. The transparency operation aimed at regaining credibility gives rise to rapid and contrasting reactions. Here, it is the race for improvised disciplinary solutions. There, it is the proposal of innovative theses, all of which resemble more an institutional rescue operation than a profound conversion,

---

[1] From the privileged post of my function as Prefect of the Congregation for Bishops, I have been able to observe closely the evolution of the situation and the extent of the purification underway.

likely inadequate to reassure the people of God and generate new vocations.

Priests feel uncomfortable in their role, more than ever misunderstood, and even often suspected *a priori* of misconduct or a double life, in a world that does not value chastity and does not believe in a definitive commitment to love. Many parish communities see their priests getting older and find that they are overburdened, overworked, and overwhelmed by their tasks and by the general atmosphere around them. In traditionally Christian countries, essential services are still offered, but the numbers are decreasing, morale is falling, and pastoral prospects remain rather bleak, despite the missionary impetus incarnated by Pope Francis and strongly proposed in his programmatic Apostolic Exhortation *Evangelii Gaudium*.

The future of priestly celibacy in question

Who in the field of ordinary pastoral care does not feel divided between two opposing feelings? For, on the one hand, we insist on missionary conversion, which should witness and generate enthusiasm; while, on the other hand, we are internally undermined by an impression of the end of the era, when the remains of a pastoral care of maintenance, familiar in Christian times but ineffective in new contexts, disappear. How can we respond adequately and adapt to the needs of evangelization, without which past practices risk falling into insignificance? Baptisms are decreasing; marriages are also decreasing; confession is disappearing, despite all efforts to restore it; few priests are available to ensure the Eucharist for all communities, and where they celebrate, few rush to feed themselves as a vital reality. How are we to awaken faith in souls and reinculturate it in a secularized world? How can we maintain the wick that still smokes, and light the fire that Christ came to cast on the earth?

These questions haunt priests and interrogate them about the meaning and limits of their own ministry. It is clear that pastoral recipes, which could stimulate communities after the *aggiornamento* of the Second Vatican Ecumenical Council, no longer meet today's problems. The enthusiasm for the liturgy, the structures of consultation at different levels, the apostolic movements, and many other realities, have given way to currents of secularization that have significantly changed the habits of priests and the demands of their ministry. Today, the Christian world of yesteryear has changed so much, and the surrounding culture is so uprooted and shaped by other values, that we struggle not only to save the essentials of the faith but to discern the customs and structures that guarantee its vitality. Hence the recurrent and increasingly critical questions about priestly celibacy.

In a world that is moving forward *etsi Deus non daretur* ("as if God does not exist"), the model of the priest at the head of a parish community seems to have failed, and his lifestyle is often no longer understood or valued. Loneliness, overwork, perils, and uncertainty about the future worry young people and motivate some to seek the religious life instead of persevering in the diocesan way, or to serve in dioceses within priestly fraternities offering more favorable conditions.[2] The priests themselves no longer feel attracted to or rewarded by their ministry, because they see the disaffection of the faithful with regard to reception of the sacraments, which is in addition to the fact that they are scattered and little known over a vast territory, where they become responsible for a region covering several former parishes. This description does not cover all situations, of course, and should be qualified according to the

---

[2] This trend can be observed in France, for example, where the proportion of priestly vocations that are directed towards the Community of Saint Martin is significant.

contexts and different degrees of secularization. Nevertheless, it describes a major trend that deeply affects the lives of priests and their efforts to adapt to the new conditions of the mission.

One could dwell longer on the difficulties of the present hour, but a pessimistic or bitter discourse would not bring anything to the cause of the Gospel. Is it possible to regain the enthusiasm of one's own vocation in the present conditions and to revive the mission of priests in a way that is humanly viable, spiritually meaningful, and pastorally effective? How can we achieve the missionary conversion that Pope Francis embodies, through the creativity and audacity that he manifests in the midst of difficulties and resistances that are no less than those experienced on the ground in dioceses and parishes?

In search of new ways in a missionary context

The Catholic Church is now at the forefront of the ecological cause with the Synod on the Amazon, which brings to the forefront the encyclical *Laudato si* and the great planetary objective of an integral human ecology. Promising dialogues are being announced, and new missionary strategies are emerging that could have a long-term impact on priestly ministry, either locally or more broadly, given the globalizing influence of a borderless media culture. Some aspire to the rapid adoption of the pastoral solution of the *viri probati*—that is, married men, heads of stable families, who could be ordained priests in order to ensure the Eucharistic celebration for dispersed indigenous communities to whom the value of celibacy seems foreign. The Synod on the Amazon is about to address this issue.[3]

---

[3] Synod of Bishops, Special Assembly for the Pan-Amazonian Region: *The Amazon: New Paths for the Church and for Integral Ecology—Instrumentum laboris*, no. 129, §2.

These prospects may be attractive to some, and cause concern elsewhere, if one considers that elements of ideology and strategy are intertwined to achieve more ambitious and important results at the universal level. Liberal, or frankly protesting, currents of thought are resurfacing to take advantage of the situation and propose reform programs that go beyond Pope Francis's intentions and orientations. The Holy Father has clearly placed the synodal operation on the Amazon under the movement of the Holy Spirit, and in an atmosphere of prayer, dialogue and openness to newness. But it relies on free discussion to ensure discernment useful for evangelization, in a context where divergent ideas on inculturation and interculturality confront not only each other but also opposing interests and forces hostile to the influence of the Church.

That being said, new paths of the future will bear evangelical fruits if they are consistent with a complete proclamation of the Gospel, *sine glosa*, which does not sacrifice anything of the permanent values of the Christian tradition. In this regard, we must certainly develop pastoral creativity attentive to the characteristics of particular cultures, but we must first verify the quality of the witness of missionaries, who can effectively transmit the faith when it permeates their entire lives and unambiguously motivates their lifestyle and evangelizing activity. If sensitivity to the ecclesial aspects of inculturation and interculturality must give rise to more advanced missionary formation, the essential part of evangelization always remains the personal and ecclesial missionary consciousness emanating from the intimate encounter with Jesus Christ, and from his call to witness to a divine Life that transcends all cultures and which, for this very reason, makes possible a peaceful encounter between the culture of the missionaries and the local culture.

In this light, seeking new ways for the evangelization of indigenous peoples in the Amazon means going beyond an approach that would stem from Amazonian worldviews, in an effort of intercultural synthesis that runs the risk of being artificial and syncretistic. The uniqueness of Jesus Christ and, to a certain extent, of the biblical culture requires a dialogue that respects cultures but is clearly oriented towards conversion to the mystery of the Incarnation of the Word. The transcendental uniqueness of this irruption of the Word into human history confers on the biblical culture a special place in the concert of nations and justifies its thorough teaching at great expense to all cultures, in order to bring them what they aspire to, and to which they carry their values and limits in order to be illuminated, healed, and assumed beyond themselves. The Holy Spirit remains the hermeneutical key to any transmission of faith from one culture to another, according to a logic that is not primarily ideas and symbols, but interpersonal communion in the diversity of situations and cultures.[4]

For, in the final analysis, evangelization is not a process of inculturation and interculturality; rather it precedes and makes possible this process, which presupposes the grace of the encounter with Christ and adherence to His Person. This grace of conversion is facilitated by the personal witness of missionaries who know in Whom they believe, and who do not confuse the proclamation of Jesus Christ with all the just causes related to the human, social, and environmental promotion of the populations to be evangelized. A unilateral emphasis on the cultural dimension sometimes leads to unfair criticism of the abuses of past history, and the reduction of evangelization to the promotion of the social dimension, to the detriment of the religious sensitivity of the

---

[4] Saint Paul VI, Apostolic Exhortation *Evangelii Nuntiandi*, no. 75: "There will never be evangelization without the action of the Holy Spirit.... It can be said that the Holy Spirit is the principal agent of evangelization: it is he who urges each one to proclaim the Gospel, and it is he who in the depths of consciousness makes the word of salvation accepted and understood (cf. Second Vatican Ecumenical Council, *Ad Gentes*, no. 4)."

populations. The Church in South America has seen some instances of the faithful deserting to sectarian communities because religious sentiment was not adequately integrated into evangelizing activity.

But behind these failures and defects lies the implicit, and not always recognized, assumption that evangelization is a question of ideas, rites, customs, values, and models, when in reality, all this is derived, consequent, incidental: The essential thing is the identity of a communion, the fruit of an encounter brought about by the Holy Spirit between the Word of the Father, Christ, and each human community and its culture. Each culture is open in principle to this encounter-communion, because of the *semina Verbi* deposited by the Creator in all His works, who aspire and walk towards their fulfillment in the encounter with the incarnate and redemptive Word. Hence the importance of the proclamation of the Word of God by the Church in the power of the Spirit and His fruit in the integral acceptance of the faith, which extends to sacramental expression.

If this reflection on evangelization is valid for the Amazon, a similar reflection applies to the "new evangelization" of the former Christendom. If it is confused with a modernization of morals and customs, in order to make Christianity more acceptable despite its historical misadventures, we are condemned to failure, and people are not fooled by superficial recipes that are proposed to them to maintain the interest of the ecclesial institution. Either the Church proposes the authentic Jesus, Who is identical to the Christ of faith, or She loses the raison d'être of Her mission, and the new powers and means managed by hostile hands will soon make it obsolete and superfluous. The current wave of persecutions augurs a difficult future for the ecclesial institution, but it purifies by bringing out heroic testimonies that clearly show the risen Christ always present and active in the heart of the world.

These considerations may seem distant and superfluous in relation to the problems of priests, their insufficient number, their misunderstood lifestyle, their loneliness and lack of fraternity, their deficient or purely functional spirituality. Yet the Church cannot deprive Herself of their services or seek substitutes for them without betraying Her mission. She does not have the right to resign Herself to a shortage of priestly and religious vocations, and to reinvent Herself with any means at Her disposal, claiming to be adequate to Her mission. Who will measure the missionary energy that priests deploy by making present Christ, Who baptizes, absolves, consecrates, and gives Himself as food, by offering to all who come His pastoral charity, which consoles the afflicted, helps the dying, visits the poor, and heals the sick? Missionary urgency challenges the whole Church and in particular religious and laity, but how can this missionary awareness be made operational, if not by showing that the priesthood of the baptized and the priesthood of priests have a common cause from the very principle and essence of the mission?

The conditions for a priestly renewal

To ask this vast question obliges us to reflect more deeply on the challenges of current missionary research, which cannot do without theology; otherwise we risk betraying the main objective of evangelization. The Holy Spirit therefore invites us, first of all, to a renewed listening and authentic theological creativity emanating from the Word of God, and led by a missionary passion that neglects nothing of the *plantatio ecclesiae* (the establishment of the Church), in the rich diversity of peoples, cultures, and worldviews. How, then, can the very idea of priesthood be placed in the more clearly explained context of the service of the Gospel in Christian communities?

This is the challenge posed by this book concerning the priesthood and celibacy. The following reflections elaborated in various circumstances approach the questions from a new point of view — but anchored in Tradition, without isolating this vocation or exalting it above the others, without reducing the diversity of vocations and charisms to a common denominator, adopting a virtually symphonic approach, seeking better to see the harmony of the different vocations that gravitate around the Catholic conception of the priesthood.

The treatises of the priesthood that speak of the presbyterate abound and constitute an indisputable richness of the ecclesial tradition. The doctrine of the episcopate, although more important, was only systematically developed recently at the Second Vatican Council, and it remains to be perfected and implemented. The permanent diaconate was restored by the last Council and is being consolidated in several regions of the Church, while still seeking its doctrinal and pastoral unity.

The reflections included here have the originality of placing the doctrine of the priesthood in a global ecclesiological context, interpreted in a sacramental and missionary perspective, starting from a Trinitarian horizon and a pneumatological vision generally absent from the classical treatises. The result from the point of view adopted is a fundamentally relational vision, which interprets in a nuptial perspective Christ's relationship to the Church, ecclesial and first of all Marian participation in the one priesthood of Christ, as well as the fundamental meaning of consecrated life as the solemn profession of baptism.

The idea of priestly mediation is first described in Christological and pneumatological terms from the Paschal Mystery. It is firstly participated in Mary, who incarnates the perfect lived experience of the baptismal priesthood. It continues in the institution of the hierarchical priesthood with its different degrees, which are essentially distinct from the common priesthood, and not only as a matter of degrees.[5] This complex and delicate question from an

---

[5] Second Vatican Council, Dogmatic Constitution on the Church, *Lumen Gentium*, no. 10: "Though they differ from one another in

ecumenical point of view receives in these pages a Trinitarian and pneumatological deepening, which radically establishes the relational nature and mutual ordination of the two participations in the one priesthood of Christ.

The question of priestly celibacy is taken up in depth in the face of the many objections that constantly challenge it and invoke its abolition. The aim here is not only to defend the traditional reasons for the discipline of the Latin Church, but to deepen them and show their relevance today and precisely in difficult contexts, where one would be tempted to put an end to a practice recognized as valid in principle, but discounted in practice, and ultimately destined to give way to other missionary and pastoral priorities.

This very synthetic overview that I have just formulated is to be found in the various contributions of this book, which are quite recent but clearly articulated according to this synthesis, whether in the conferences on the episcopate, the priesthood, celibacy, the relationship between Mary and the priesthood, the relationship between the common priesthood and the hierarchical priesthood, priestly spirituality, all unified by a pneumatological contribution that I would dare to describe as systematic, even if the Holy Spirit does not allow Himself to be locked into any system.

The reader will notice that the vision proposed here goes off the beaten track by taking into account the human sciences but not allowing itself to be determined by them, in order to main-tain a theological, methodologically vital, and prudent point of view, in order to avoid the Catholic doctrine of the priesthood and celibacy being traced back to the needs felt or supposed in certain extreme pastoral situations. An indisputable apostolic tradition of

essence and not only in degree, the common priesthood of the faith-ful and the ministerial or hierarchical priesthood are nonetheless interrelated: Each of them in its own special way is a participation in the one priesthood of Christ."

total continence regarding the requirements of the *vita apostolica* for the Apostles and their successors, as well as for priests and deacons once ordained, which has been preserved with ups and downs in the Latin tradition, cannot be relativized in the name of pastoral imperatives that sometimes hide the real problem.

For, in the end, the decline in priestly vocations depends on many statistical, cultural, and ecclesiological factors, but it cannot be denied that it also depends, and undoubtedly first of all, on a crisis of faith.[6] Fewer families, the revaluation of marriage and sexuality, the reintegration of the priesthood into a new ecclesiological framework — all this plays a significant role, but the crisis of faith, linked to a Christological and therefore Trinitarian deficit, undermines at the root the decisive motivation to respond to a call to leave everything to follow Christ. If this is true, it must be anticipated that the Church's abandonment of Her discipline of celibacy for Her ministers of the second degree of the priesthood would have an incalculable and quite predictable impact

---

[6] See Benedict XVI, Apostolic Letter in the form of *motu proprio Porta Fidei*, October 11, 2011: "Since the beginning of my ministry as Successor of Peter, I have recalled the need to rediscover the path of faith in order to highlight ever more clearly the joy and renewed enthusiasm of the encounter with Christ. In the homily at Mass for the inauguration of my pontificate I said: 'The Church as a whole, and the pastors in it, must, like Christ, set out on a journey, to lead men out of the desert, to the place of life, to friendship with the Son of God, to him who gives us life, life in fullness.' Christians are now often more interested in the social, cultural and political consequences of their commitment, continuing to think of faith as an obvious presupposition of living together. Indeed, this presupposition is not only no longer such, but often even denied. Whereas in the past it was possible to recognize a unitary cultural fabric, widely accepted in its reference to the contents of the faith and the values inspired by it, today this no longer seems to be the case in large sectors of society, because of a deep crisis of faith that has affected many people."

on vocations to consecrated life in all its forms. If celibacy is no longer a decisive value for the exercise of priestly ministry, religious life itself is devalued and relegated to the background in favor of the priestly function. It would be appropriate to ask the following question: What remains of celibate consecrated life in communities of Protestant tradition?

Today more than ever, the pastoral wisdom of the Church and theological creativity must overcome a rationalist mentality that dominates many academic circles and pastoral test beds, in order to revive the vocational culture and the future of priestly ministry with a coherent vision of celibacy as a state of life[7] that is capable of inspiring, motivating and empowering men not only to act with contagious conviction, but also to suffer rejection and persecution based on the witness of the apostolic life of its origins. The proclamation of the Word of God and the celebration of the sacraments have another impact when the minister's faith is first proclaimed by his state of life, which gives his preaching a weight or fire, gushing out from the Spirit, from a life completely given to his Lord in ministry. This is attested to in the Amazon by priests who experience being welcomed and integrated into local communities precisely because of their celibacy. Should we not, then, at least ask ourselves whether it would be counterproductive for evangelization to introduce an alternative to priestly celibacy?

The apostolic life of the origins has lost none of its relevance: As the Spouse of humanity, Jesus instituted the witness of total continence, and what He demanded of His Apostles and their successors, remains the form of evangelical life that incarnates the Trinitarian Communion offered to married humanity. This is evidenced by the state of life of bishops, which over the centuries has

---

[7] See Hans Urs von Balthasar, *L'état de vie chrétien* (Johannes Verlag, 2016; original German 1977).

remained unchanging and unchallenged in both East and West. It also remains the ideal for priests who participate in the second degree of the mystery of the priesthood, as representatives of Christ the Head and Spouse, wishing to love the Church, the Bride of the same Love with which She is loved by Her Lord and Spouse.[8]

The present hour of the Church "going out" would not, in my opinion, benefit from reducing the requirements of the priesthood in the name of regional cultural and pastoral imperatives, in order to ensure so-called essential services that are not essential, or are no longer felt as such, in the countries from which the missionaries come. It would be better to rely on a renewed proclamation of the kerygma, that is, of the Word of God, Which is Christ, to make the true believer see in Him, with the eyes of the Spirit, the kenosis of God in history, which plunges him into an abyss of adoration and unlimited availability, so that this Love does not remain unanswered, so that this Love rightly demands everything, so that it makes him totally in love with Jesus and eager to identify himself with Him in all humility and truth, for the love of Love.

The mission in the Amazon, as elsewhere, cannot progress on the basis of more or less ideological slogans, based on valid but secondary considerations in relation to the essential objective of evangelization: to give Christ.[9] The new ways of mission to compose

---

[8] See Saint John Paul II, Post-Synodal Apostolic Exhortation *Pastores Dabo Vobis*, no. 29: "The Church, as Spouse of Jesus Christ, wants to be loved by the priest in the total and exclusive way in which Jesus Christ Head and Spouse loved her."

[9] Cf. Saint John Paul II, Apostolic Letter *Tertio Millennio Adveniente*, no. 6: "We touch here on the essential point that differentiates Christianity from other religions, in which man's search for God was expressed from the very beginning. In Christianity, the starting point is the Incarnation of the Word. Here, it is no longer only man who seeks God, but it is God who comes in person to speak to man about himself and show him the way that will allow him to

an indigenous face of the Church must start, there as elsewhere, from the Word of God contemplated in all its beauty, which can delight people of all cultures and inspire them with the desire to embrace celibacy as a witness of love, in a state of life that implies an overcoming of the values of the first creation by virtue of the grace of the new creation in Christ.[10]

For the promotion of the integral priestly vocation

The above considerations are in no way intended to hinder the momentum and creativity of the Synod on the Amazon, which rightly proposes a bold search for new ways of inculturation and

reach him. This is what the prologue to John's Gospel proclaims: 'No one has ever seen God; the only Son, who is turned to the bosom of the Father, has made him known' (1:18). The Incarnate Word is therefore the fulfillment of the aspiration present in all the religions of humanity: this fulfillment is the work of God and exceeds all human expectations. It is a mystery of grace. In Christ, religion is no longer a 'search for God as if groping' (cf. Acts 17:27), but a response of faith to God who reveals himself: a response in which man speaks to God as to his Creator and Father; a response made possible by this one Man who is at the same time the con-substantial Word to the Father, in whom God speaks to every man and in whom every man is enabled to answer to God. Moreover, in this Man, the whole creation responds to God. Jesus Christ is the new beginning of everything: in him, everything is found, everything is welcomed and returned to the Creator from whom it originated. In this way, Christ is the realization of the aspiration of all the world's religions and, by this very fact, he is the only and definitive outcome."

[10] This observation applies to the priesthood, and even more so to consecrated life, which also risks being understood in a functional way, to the detriment of the fundamental and prophetic meaning of consecration to God. Cf. Congregation for Institutes of Consecrated Life and Societies of Apostolic Life, *Starting Afresh from Christ: A Renewed Commitment to Consecrated Life in the Third Millennium* (Vatican Publishing House, 2002).

missionary presence, so that the Church may acquire there the face that corresponds to integral evangelization. These critical reflections are intended, above all, to deepen its essential purpose and to warn against the danger of confining oneself to superficial creativity. Let us avoid the temptation to trade the evangelical boldness of the great saints who inspire Pope Francis (Francis of Assisi, Ignatius of Loyola, Thérèse of the Child Jesus, the Holy Family of Nazareth) for do-it-yourself approach utilizing uncertain human innovations that risk weakening the salt of the Gospel instead of making the Church more evangelical and radiant in and through local cultures, because She is more committed in all Her members to a nuptial relationship with Christ. This objective will be achieved in the medium and long term if the integral priestly vocation—that is, the communion between the common priesthood of the baptized and the hierarchical priesthood of the ministers of the Gospel—is promoted with great care.

Whether it is directing families to the Sacrament of Marriage, and protecting women and children from violence; whether it is with young people exposed nowadays to all distractions and deviances, and condemned to idleness or wandering on the web; be it in the workplace, at leisure, or in public life, vigorous preaching and contemplative attendance to the Word of God must generate a vocational culture in which life itself is understood as a vocation and thus put into a perspective of dialogue, Covenant, and mission. Such a vocational culture presupposes a pastoral care of vocations articulated and animated by, among others, single priests who are happy to be so despite all the failures and all the noise against them.

These are priests who are authentic "friends of the Bridegroom" detached from themselves and passionate about the Gospel; kerygmatic and pastoral priests, capable of accompanying people and communities with mercy and discernment after the example of

Friends of the Bridegroom

Pope Francis; priests paternally supported by their bishop and by the concrete fraternity of their presbyterium or community of belonging; priests trained in the "spirituality of communion," who know how to appreciate and promote the charisms with which the Spirit enriches believers. Finally, priests whose quest for holiness is not rigid and narcissistic, but all leavened with pastoral charity, and therefore oriented towards the service of the holiness of the people of God.

This is what a synod on the indigenous face of the Church in the Amazon cannot take for granted but could promote by being fully part of the vocational movement of *Christus vivit*, the post-synodal Apostolic Exhortation of Pope Francis addressed to the young and to all the people of God. This means placing prayer, the invocation of the Holy Spirit, theological reflection, and pastoral creativity in the foreground. It is not only about inculturation and interculturality, but it should be, first of all, about vocational culture, if we want to achieve the great objective of an authentically Catholic, local and particular ecclesial community in salvific mission through an integral human ecology founded on Christ.

Moreover, the objective of this Synod cannot be closely limited to this geographical space; it must integrate the planetary singularity of the Amazon into an adequate anthropological research, marked out by Saint John Paul II, and responding to the culture of death that has now taken hold of the planet on the ethical, cultural, environmental, and geopolitical levels. To save the Amazon, with its environmental, human, and ecclesial cultural riches, is to save the hope of humanity, which learns, for better or for worse, that "everything is interconnected" and that its future depends on dialogue within the "common house" inspired by the Church's social doctrine, with a view to a globalization of solidarity. Like the missionary passion that animates current research on the Amazon, Christ's "missionary disciples," committed in the name of His Love in a state of consecrated life, single or married, are the most motivated and equipped to save the hope of humanity by embodying together the witness of the Holy Spirit, "the Principal Agent" and "the end of evangelization" that sows the joy of the Gospel in every wind:

> Jesus wants evangelizers who proclaim the good news not only with words, but above all by a life transfigured by God's presence.... How I long to find the right words to stir up enthusiasm for a new chapter of evangelization full of fervour, joy, generosity, courage, boundless love and attraction! Yet I realize that no words of encouragement will be enough unless the fire of the Holy Spirit burns in our hearts. A spirit-filled evangelization is one guided by the Holy Spirit, for he is the soul of the Church called to proclaim the Gospel. Before offering some spiritual motivations and suggestions, I once more invoke the Holy Spirit. I implore him to come and renew the Church, to stir and impel her to go forth boldly to evangelize all peoples.... Yet there is no greater freedom than that of allowing oneself to be guided by the Holy Spirit, renouncing the attempt to plan and control everything to the last detail, and instead letting him enlighten, guide and direct us, leading us wherever he wills. The Holy Spirit knows well what is needed in every time and place. This is what it means to be mysteriously fruitful![11]

---

[11] Pope Francis, Apostolic Exhortation *Evangelii Gaudium*, nos. 259-261, 280.

Part 1

Common Priesthood and Ministerial Priesthood: The Meaning of the Priestly Vocation

The one who has the bride is the bridegroom; the best man, who stands and listens to him, rejoices greatly at the bridegroom's voice. So this joy of mine has been made complete. He must increase; I must decrease."

— John 3:29–30

Chapter 1

Towards a Renewal of the
Priesthood for Our Time

I am honored and deeply grateful to receive a doctorate in Divinity *honoris causa* from Saint Mary's Seminary and the University of Baltimore. In return, I offer this theological meditation as a tribute to the 225 years of service to priestly formation in the United States rendered by the Society of Saint-Sulpice. My sincere congratulations!

The organizers have kindly allowed me to choose the topic of my remarks. I had initially considered speaking to you about the Church's reflection on the family during the last few years and about the need—which is acutely felt in our present cultural circumstances—for a nuptial outpouring of the Holy Spirit. But since this latter point is already extensively treated in the Apostolic Exhortation *Amoris Laetitia*, my next idea was to talk about its proper pastoral implementation. As I thought about this, I was struck by the notion that such an implementation requires a nuptial outpouring of the Holy Spirit on the other states of life as well—an outpouring needed to guarantee the convergence and coherence of the Church's witness.

I have accordingly chosen to talk about the priesthood, given the central role it plays in any reform of the Church. Instead of approaching my topic in isolation, however, I would like to discuss it in the framework of the Trinitarian, Eucharistic, and nuptial ecclesiology whose development was launched by the Second Vatican Ecumenical Council. As the Dogmatic Constitution *Lumen Gentium* teaches, "Though they differ from one another in essence and not only in degree, the common priesthood of the faithful and the ministerial or hierarchical priesthood are nonetheless interrelated: Each of them in its own special way is a participation in the one priesthood of Christ."[12]

For over twenty-five years, I have been reflecting on this essential difference between, and mutual ordering of, the two modes of sharing in Christ's one and only priesthood. As I see it, conciliar and postconciliar ecclesiology has not yet fully integrated this teaching. Note, in fact, that the sentence I just cited occurs at the end of *Lumen Gentium*'s section on the common priesthood, which the document treats first, in chapter 2 on the People of God, in order, it seems, to safeguard the specificity of the ministerial priesthood. The sentence itself is laden with theological, pastoral, and ecumenical implications, implications that theologians have by no means exhausted, the postconciliar boom in ecclesiology notwithstanding.

The claim of a difference in kind, and not merely in degree, [between the two modes of priesthood] has caused much ink to flow on the part of defenders and challengers alike. The difference in question is intimately bound up with the Catholic understanding of the priesthood, which, since the Council of Trent, has been particularly concerned to refute the Protestant denial of the ordained ministry, sometimes, it must be admitted, to the detriment of the common priesthood. The Second Vatican Council reestablished

---

[12] Second Vatican Council, Dogmatic Constitution on the Church, *Lumen Gentium*, no. 10. Hereafter: *LG*.

a certain balance in that it restored the dignity of the common priesthood while also safeguarding the irreducibility of the ministerial. This recalibration is of a piece with the dynamic development of the apostolate of the laity, the universal call to holiness, and the new awareness of mission on the part of the Church. At the same time, it also harmonizes with the Council's ample vision of the Church as the Sacrament of Salvation, a vision that, as the first lines of the Constitution already make plain, connects two themes: participation in Trinitarian communion and the unity of the human race. It seems to me, however, that this comprehensive renewal in ecclesiology calls for a systematic effort to approach the priesthood in the Church in light of a renewed pneumatology and Trinitarian theology. It is just this approach that is the subject matter of the following remarks.

I propose to begin, then, by discussing the Holy Spirit's relationship to the priesthood of Christ in the Trinitarian economy of the Incarnation and the Paschal Mystery. I will then go on to speak about the relationship between the Holy Spirit and the priesthood in the Church in terms of nuptiality. Finally, I will say something about the ultimate foundation of the essential difference and the correlation between the two modes of participating in the one and only priesthood of Christ in the Church.[13]

I admit from the outset that my subject is not obviously in the forefront of the burning ecclesial issues of our time, and that it

---

[13] My reflection here will be of a systematic and synthetic character. For a fuller development of the topic, I refer to some of my other publications: *Divine Likeness: Toward a Trinitarian Anthropology of the Family* (Wm. B. Eerdmans Publishing, 2006); *Mystery and Sacrament of Love. A Theology of Marriage and the Family for the New Evangelization* (Wm. B. Eerdmans Publishing, 2015); *The Relevance and Future of the Second Vatican Council* (Ignatius Press, 2013).

might seem a bit abstract, not to mention remote from the political dramas of the moment. I am convinced, however, that a deeper understanding of the priesthood, in its twofold form, remains vitally important for the Church's testimony of communion, for the nurturing of vocations, for the initial and continuing formation of priests, as well as for ecumenism and the pastoral and missionary conversion so vigorously promoted by Pope Francis for the reform of the Church.

I. The Holy Spirit and the priesthood of Jesus Christ

An important first step in our reflection is to recall the Trinitarian pattern structuring the opening of the Dogmatic Constitution *Lumen Gentium*, which describes both the Protagonists of, and the stages in, God's design. The description begins thus: "The eternal Father, by a free and hidden plan of His own wisdom and goodness, created the whole world. His plan was to raise men to a participation in the divine life."[14] To this end, He sent His Son, "the image of the invisible God, the first-born of every creature" (Col 1:15), in whom we are predestined to reflect His image (Rom 8:29). And we are to do so in the communion of the Church, which has already been made manifest "by the outpouring of the Spirit" and "at the end of time ... will gloriously achieve [its] completion."[15]

Christ, then, came to fulfill the Father's will. He came to make us the Father's children by His obedience unto death on the Cross, an obedience that wrought our Redemption and inaugurated the Kingdom of God through His Resurrection from the dead. This Kingdom becomes manifest "as often as the sacrifice of the Cross ... is celebrated on the altar [and] the work of our redemption is

[14] *LG*, no. 2.
[15] Ibid.

carried on, [for] in the Sacrament of the Eucharistic bread, the unity of all believers who form one body in Christ is both expressed and brought about (cf. 1 Cor 10:17)."[16]

Lumen Gentium continues: "When the work which the Father gave the Son to do on earth (cf. Jn 17:4) was accomplished, the Holy Spirit was sent on the day of Pentecost in order that He might continually sanctify the Church, and thus, all those who believe would have access through Christ in one Spirit to the Father (cf. Eph 2:18)."[17] "The Spirit dwells in the Church and in the hearts of the faithful, as in a temple.[18] In them He prays on their behalf and bears witness to the fact that they are adopted sons.[19] The Church … He both equips and directs with hierarchical and charismatic gifts and adorns with His fruits (Eph 4:11-12; 1 Cor 12:4; Gal 5:22)." Finally, "He renews it and leads it to perfect union with its Spouse." "Thus, the Church has been seen as 'a people made one with the unity of the Father, the Son and the Holy Spirit.'"[20]

Lumen Gentium thus presents the divine plan in Trinitarian sequence: God the Father sends His Son, and the Son's death and Resurrection, in their turn, inaugurate the gift of the Holy Spirit. Note how this account finds its natural conclusion in a remarkable pneumatological synthesis firmly rooted in Holy Scripture. An important point that emerges in this context is that humanity — having been created by the Father, redeemed by Christ, and sanctified by the Holy Spirit — already participates in, and is destined to rejoice fully in, the communion of the divine Persons.

---

[16] *LG*, no. 3.
[17] *LG*, no. 4.
[18] Cf. 1 Cor 3:16; 6:19.
[19] Cf. Gal 4:6; Rom 8:15-16, 26.
[20] *LG*, no. 4.

Friends of the Bridegroom

Christ's priesthood is an integral part of this Trinitarian plan; it is the central mediation of the divine communion that both constitutes the Church and sets Her up as a "sign" and "instrument" of salvation in the sight of the nations. Before going on to examine the relationship between the two modes of ecclesial participation in Christ's priesthood, let us first reflect on the theological depths of this priesthood itself and on its relation to the gift of the Holy Spirit. We will approach this question in light of the Trinitarian background we have just sketched.

Let us begin with a fundamental premise that may seem obvious at first but is actually full of sometimes overlooked implications: The priesthood of Jesus Christ is nothing other than His very divine-human being, itself a mystery of Covenant (*connubium*), seen in its totality as a process of incarnating the Trinitarian Love to the end—that is, the end reached in the Paschal Mystery and the Eucharist. The priesthood of Jesus Christ is not simply one particular item on the list of activities exercised by the Son of God, Who came in the flesh. His priesthood is the redemptive mediation of His incarnate Person, Whose obedience of Love to the point of death and descent into Hell opens to the Resurrection and the gift of the Holy Spirit. Christ's priesthood is not dynastic, levitical, or institutional, as is the case in other religions or even in the tradition of ancient Israel, where priesthood is based on membership in a caste or on cultic duties of one kind or another. Jesus did not belong to the tribe of Levi, nor did He refer to Himself in the Gospels as a priest—a fact, however, that does not prevent the Letter to the Hebrews from recapitulating the significance of His mission in fully priestly terms. Jesus is a layman who emerges from the prophetic tradition and suffers the lot of the prophets, though His tragic destiny, unlike theirs, ends in eschatological victory with His Resurrection from the dead.

"The Gospel of God," to cite Saint Paul's solemn words in the Letter to the Romans, "concerns the Son of God, sprung from David's line according to the flesh, but established according to the Spirit as Son of God in power by his resurrection from the dead, Jesus Christ our Lord."[21] This Lord Jesus Christ, then, is confirmed by the Holy Spirit as Son of God in power, as victor over death, and as High Priest of the New Covenant. By the same token, the Holy Spirit also confirms the value of Christ's sacrifice as an oblation of His own blood offered "once for all," i.e., in such a way as to bring about a definitive liberation and purification.[22] By its very nature, in other words, Christ's priesthood, crowned as it is by the Gift of the Spirit, is an existential mediation, at once human and divine, that reconciles the world with God and gives it access to the communion that is the Trinity. This gift is communicated to the Church precisely by the gift of the Spirit of Life and Truth. This is why, once the Son has completed His redemptive work, it is now time for the Spirit to enter the scene as Sanctifier, to help appropriating the gift, to recall the gift of the Father and the Son, and to enliven the Church's faith and life, all as the fundamental Agent of Her participation in the priesthood of Christ.

At this point, however, we must note a particular feature of the relationship between Christ and the Spirit. During the successively unfolding course of Jesus' life, this relation, this intimate, active-passive *connubium* and collaboration, undergoes an inversion. The first phase of Jesus' existence gives evidence of a more active role for the Spirit, to whom Jesus freely submits in obedience to the Father as He follows out the path leading to His Hour. The Gospels, in fact, bear witness that Jesus was "conceived by the Holy Spirit"; that He was driven into the desert by the Spirit; that He was guided

[21] Rom 1:4.
[22] Heb 9:12-14.

and inspired by the same Spirit in His preaching and miracles; and that He was subjected by this Spirit's help to the supreme test of redemptive obedience, culminating in death on the Cross. "When Jesus had taken the wine, he said, 'It is accomplished,' and, bowing his head, he handed over his Spirit."[23]

At the end of his earthly journey, the incarnate Word's passivity—or active receptivity—vis-à-vis the Spirit inverts again into an active possession of, and freedom to send, the Spirit that is grounded in His, Christ's, Resurrection from the dead. Standing in the midst of His disciples gathered in the Upper Room on the evening of the first Easter, "he breathed upon them and said 'Receive the Holy Spirit. Whose sins you forgive will be forgiven them. Whose sins you bind will be bound.'"[24] Having been receptive to the Spirit during His earthly life, Christ now becomes an active subject Who sends the Spirit at will, inasmuch as the event of the Resurrection has filled His humanity with the plenitude of the same Holy Spirit.[25]

The difference in the ordering of Christ's relation to the Spirit before and after Easter, then, is not without importance for His priesthood, the very purpose of which, after all, is to glorify the Father by pouring out the Spirit of eternal life upon all flesh.[26] This is why Christ lets Himself be incarnated by the Spirit and remains open to receive Him throughout His earthly journey; it is why He lets Himself be shaped by the Spirit and filled by the Spirit's fullness, so that, as Lord of the Church and of human history, He might communicate this plenitude without measure. We see, then, a coincidence between Christ's priesthood and the self-opening

[23] Jn 19:30.
[24] Jn 20:22-23.
[25] Cf. Jn 7:37-38; 16:7-15.
[26] Cf. Jn 17:1-2.

of the Trinitarian mystery in His historical and paschal existence: sustained by the Spirit, the Son incarnates His eternal generation in His temporal obedience, which culminates in the supreme Trinitarian moment of His death. Here, the Father glorifies Christ's obedience by the Spirit, who raises Him from the dead and establishes Him at the same time as Lord of the universe, as Bridegroom of the Church, and as Savior of the human race.[27]

II. The Holy Spirit and priesthood in the Church

Christ's priesthood, we have said, culminates in the Gift of the Holy Spirit, Whom He receives from His Father and pours out upon all flesh by virtue of His Paschal Mystery. But how does this Spirit manifest His own mission and His own mediation in relation to the Church and Her participation in Christ's priesthood? The answer depends on grasping the following: Having intimately accompanied the incarnation of Trinitarian love in the flesh of the Word, the Spirit continues this incarnation in the Church, though now in His own proper, ecclesial mode. This mode, moreover, is distinct from the singular mode of the incarnate Word; it reflects the Spirit's being, His procession from the communion of the Father and the Son. The Spirit is Communion-in-Person;[28] it is He Who unites Father and Son, while distinguishing and confirming Them, in the Trinity of Love. As Communion-in-Person, then, the Spirit incarnates Trinitarian Love in the economy in line with His own properly ecclesial and sacramental mode. He universalizes Christ's

---

[27] I am indebted for this and other points to Hans Urs von Balthasar, especially to his Johannine-inspired pneumatological Christology. Cf. *Theo-Drama III: The Dramatis Personae: The Person in Christ* (San Francisco: Ignatius Press, 1998); *Theo-Logic III: The Spirit of Truth* (San Francisco: Ignatius Press, 2005).

[28] Cf. Saint John Paul II, Encyclical Letter *Dominum et Vivificantem*, no. 10.

Incarnation in the Eucharist while giving Christ an extended body, the Church, which is both Christ's Body and Bride.

We could say, then, that the Spirit "buries" Himself afresh in the womb of the Church, from the moment that Christ's body is given up and His blood shed for our sake. This body and blood is the "seed" placed in the Church's womb; it is the ultimate incarnation of the Word, which the Virgin of Sorrows receives into her faith at the foot of the Cross, just as she once received the angel's word at the Annunciation. Here, where the Incarnation is received wholly and unreservedly by the Immaculate Virgin, the Holy Spirit presides over, and guarantees, the entire action. He sustains from within Mary's total consent to crucified Love, the painful fecundation that bears fruit in an expansion of her motherhood: the Mother of Jesus becomes the Mother of the Church. Throughout the entire process of Trinitarian Love's total incarnation, Mary, the New Eve, gives her limitless, unreserved assent, so that in her the High Priest of the New Covenant unites the Church with the priestly and nuptial outpouring of the Spirit. In so doing, He manifests to the world His Church's identity as the Bride of the Lamb and the Temple of the Spirit, as a priestly people and a royal priesthood, and as the Sacrament of Salvation.

The Holy Spirit's proper mode of incarnating Love in the communion of persons manifests Love in the Church as an "exchange of gifts" shaped, in each case, by His personhood and the distinctive nature of the different sacraments. This also holds for the sacrament we are concerned with here — namely, the Sacrament of Orders, which constitutes the hierarchical structure of the Church. In so doing, it guarantees that ecclesial *communio*, far from reducing it to a mere fraternal association of otherwise indistinguishable members, is first and foremost a sacramental participation in Trinitarian communion. For the Holy Spirit does not become present in the Church as a detached and autonomous figure; since He proceeds from the Father and the Son as Communion-in-Person, His action reproduces the order and distinction—that is, the communion—of the Trinitarian processions in the Church. Pastors and faithful, therefore, find themselves united not only by a basic fraternity resting on the foundation of Baptism, but also by specific relations founded on the "gifts" and "charisms" structuring ecclesial communion for the sake of its Trinitarian witness and the incarnation of this witness in concrete persons. The Spirit's presence and action in the Church, then, prolong the incarnation of Trinitarian Love in the ecclesial mode proper to Him, glorifying God and God's created partner in the communion of Love.

The foregoing requires that the Church's members generously welcome the Spirit of communion in all its forms—filial, fraternal, nuptial, and paternal—so as to bear witness to Christ by participating in His priesthood after the manner indicated by the Apostle Paul in Romans and Ephesians: "I therefore exhort you, brethren, in the name of God's mercy, to offer yourselves as a living sacrifice, holy and pleasing to God, your reasonable worship."[29] "Be imitators of God, since you are his beloved children. Live in love as Christ loved us and gave himself up to us as an oblation and a victim, as a sweet-smelling fragrance."[30] "Be submissive to one another out of consideration for Christ," and "Husbands, love your wives, as Christ loved the Church and gave himself up for her."[31]

In a word, the incarnation of Trinitarian Love is prolonged in the Church, where it continues to be what it was in Christ: a covenantal and nuptial mystery. The priesthood of Christ, the Bridegroom, unfolds ecclesially in a new mode that is simultaneously pneumatological and sacramental—the mode, namely, of

[29] Rom 12:1.
[30] Eph 5:1.
[31] Eph 5:25.

fruitful communion. This commits the Church to live according to the Spirit, so that, by offering Herself to be cleansed, purified, transformed, and made all beautiful by Christ,[32] She may share in His priesthood as the Spouse of the victorious Lamb Who was slain: as *Sacramentum Trinitatis*, the Sacrament of the Trinity.

III. The ultimate foundation of the difference and correlation between the two modes of participation in Christ's priesthood in the Church

We are now ready to return to the precise question concerning the relation between the common priesthood of the baptized and the ministerial priesthood exercised by the Church's hierarchy. What we have said thus far has illumined and clarified the Holy Spirit's role in the Trinitarian plan for incarnating Love in the singular mode proper to the Word made flesh and in the ecclesial-sacramental mode proper to the Spirit acting in the Church, all according to the content of Christ's own High-Priestly prayer: "That all may be one, Father, as we are one, Thou in me and I in Thee. That they may be one in us so that the world might believe that Thou has sent me."[33]

A Trinitarian ecclesiology serious about shedding light on the twofold gift of baptismal and ministerial participation in Christ's priesthood begins with the conviction that God gives Himself as what He is: Three distinct Persons in one nature. Now, according to the Revelation of Holy Scripture,[34] the divine nature is nothing other than the divine Love subsisting in three absolutely correlative Persons. Three Persons who distinguish Themselves in Love by Their manner of relating to one another according to Their

[32] Eph 5:24-27.
[33] Jn 17:21.
[34] 1 Jn 4:16.

respective origin: the Lover, the Beloved, and Love, that is: the Father, Love's Source and Principle; the Son, Who comes forth from Him as the One uniquely begotten of Love; and the Spirit, Who proceeds from the Father[35] as the substantial fruit of His Love in response to the Love of the Son. The mode proper to the Spirit in Trinitarian Love is to unite in distinguishing: He seals the unity of Love in God by Himself proceeding from the Father and the Son as Love. In this way, He confirms the distinction and consubstantial unity of the three divine Persons. This is why the Spirit is called "the Spirit of Truth" in Saint John. It is He Who crowns the consubstantiality of the Three as Love. For the same reason, He is also called the Spirit of Love, or the Holy Spirit, terms that can be applied to Him as proper names inasmuch as He personally seals and crowns the holiness of God, which is to say, God's essence as Love.

The Church's participation in this Gift of God—and it is the whole God Who gives Himself in His entirety—takes visible form in an exchange of gifts bringing divine and human persons into intimate communion, thanks to the gifts and implications of Baptism, the Eucharist, and Orders (without forgetting, of course, the other sacraments that build up the Church as Christ's Body and Bride). While the Church's pastors and faithful rejoice in the unity given by their common Baptism, they also meet face-to-face through the outpouring of the nuptial Spirit, Who makes them capable of other relations of communion as well. The Church's pastors represent, in fact, Christ as Head and Bridegroom of the Church and can act *in persona Christi*,[36] especially through the forgiveness of sins and

---

[35] Jn 15:26.

[36] Cf. Second Vatican Council, Decree on Priestly Life and Ministry, *Presbyterorum Ordinis*, 2; Saint John Paul II, Apostolic Exhortation *Pastores Dabo Vobis*, 33; Saint John Paul II, *Pastores Gregis*, 7: "Christ is the primordial icon of the Father and the manifestation of his merciful presence among men and women. The Bishop, who acts

the offering of the Eucharistic Sacrifice. By means of tokens such as these, the ecclesial community recognizes in the presence and ministry of its pastors a sign of God's initiative in His nuptial relation with redeemed humanity. This profoundly biblical dimension of nuptiality, which is anything but merely metaphorical, completes and corrects what might otherwise look like authoritarianism in an exclusive reliance on the concept of *in persona Christi Capitis*. But let us continue to clarify further the theological foundation and pneumatological structuring of the Church's share in the Trinitarian relations.

On the one hand, the common priesthood of the baptized expresses their participation in Christ's divine sonship, which as such includes His mediation of the Spirit: "By baptism into his death, then, we have been buried with him, so that, just as Christ was raised from the dead by the glory of the Father, we, too, might live in newness of life."[37] This participation in Christ's priesthood as children of the Father and as brothers and sisters, implies a new life according to Christ's Spirit, since the baptized are indwelt by the same radiant glory that raised up Christ—namely, the Holy Spirit.[38] As the Spirit fills them with His power, He equips them as Christ's witnesses.

On the other hand, the ministerial, or hierarchical, priesthood expresses Christ's mediation insofar as He represents the Father—insofar, then, as He is the Father's minister and Word Who has no desire for food other than to fulfill the Father's will. In virtue of this representation of the Father, Christ pours out the Spirit, Whom He receives from the Father in response to His,

in the person and in the name of Christ himself, becomes in the Church entrusted to him a living sign of the Lord Jesus, Shepherd and Spouse, Teacher and High Priest of the Church."

[37] Rom 6:4; 12:1.
[38] Cf. Rom 8.

Christ's, own sacrificial and Eucharistic offering. This is why He institutes the ministerial priesthood and the Eucharist simultaneously at the Last Supper.

A few moments ago, we mentioned Christ's relation to the Spirit in His pre- and post-paschal existence. At this point, we need to take a further step and draw out the Trinitarian foundation of the essential difference between the two modes of priesthood in the Church. Christ's priesthood consists in revealing the Father, in reconciling the sinful world with God, and in giving the Spirit for the sanctification of humanity. He does all of this in a twofold manner: on the one hand, as the incarnate Son, Who obeys the Father to the point of breathing forth the Holy Spirit with His own last breath; on the other hand, as the representative of the Father in virtue of the *exousia* of and over the Spirit that He receives from the Father in rising from the dead. Hence the difference between the two modes: The baptismal priesthood is filial in nature; it bears the fruit of the Spirit through the obedience of love. The ministerial priesthood, on the other hand, is paternal in nature; it communicates the Spirit of the Father, which is to say, His merciful and jealous Love as the Bridegroom of humanity, Who desires to save all men in Christ. This latter aspect is, to repeat, important for countering the all-too-common perception of authority as a "clerical power" rather than as a tender and merciful "paternity" in deep communion with the maternity of the Church, serving the growth of the children of God.

In my opinion, the fact that the mediation of the Spirit comes in two forms, the paternal and the filial, constitutes the Trinitarian foundation both of the essential difference and of the existential correlation between the two modes of participation. One mode — the baptismal — is directly tied to the life of sonship, while the other mode — the ministerial — proceeds from the paternal origin of Christ's one and only priesthood.

Friends of the Bridegroom

The foregoing Trinitarian approach confirms and reinforces the difference and correlation between the two forms of priesthood, while also offering a fundamental clarification of the meaning of priesthood as such: It is a mediation of the Holy Spirit. We see this on the side of the common priesthood, in that the baptized enjoy the gift of divine life through sanctifying grace and their various charisms; they walk towards the Father upheld by Christ, even carried by Him, as He returns to the same Father in the Spirit. They, too, are priests, first of all simply by being sons and daughters of God, Who, in the Spirit, offer the world to the Father in a sacrifice of praise. According to Vatican Council II, their filial priesthood commits them to bear witness to this same Spirit and to communicate Him through the exercise of their priesthood in "receiving the sacraments, in prayer and thanksgiving, in the witness of a holy life, and by self-denial and active charity."[39] In so doing, they "penetrat[e] … the temporal order through the spirit of the Gospel … like leaven."[40]

As for the ministerial priesthood, Christ's ministers represent the paternal authority of the divine Bridegroom, the Father from Whom the nuptial Spirit of the Risen One proceeds. As such, they are ordained for the service of the common priesthood of the baptized through the proclamation of the Word, the gift of the sacraments, and the pastoral ministry of unity in the community of the Church. They sacramentally communicate the Spirit of Trinitarian life as a Love that pardons, heals, blesses, enlivens, and sanctifies, thus building up the Church as the Body and Bride of Christ through the daily Pentecost of Eucharistic communion. In both modes, whether through the ascending mediation of the

---

[39] LG, 10, §2.
[40] Second Vatican Council, Decree on the Apostolate of the Laity, *Apostolicam Actuositatem*, no. 2.

common priesthood, whereby the baptized glorify God and intercede for the world, or through the descending mediation of the hierarchical ministry, the fruit is the same: an outpouring of the Spirit, Who confirms and augments the harmonious convergence of the two ways of participating in Christ's priesthood in the Church, so that, as the conciliar Constitution on the Liturgy explains, "Christ ... always associates the Church with Himself in this great work wherein God is perfectly glorified and men are sanctified. The Church is His beloved Bride who calls to her Lord, and through Him offers worship to the Eternal Father."[41]

Thus far, we have been approaching the priesthood in terms of a Trinitarian ecclesiology presented in a pneumatological key. We now need to complete this approach by reflecting on the Church's charismatic dimension, which is co-essential with, and complementary to, the relation between ordained ministers and the lay faithful. *Lumen Gentium* introduces the theme in number 4, where we read that the Spirit, Who gathers the Church "in communion and in works of ministry,... both equips and directs [Her] with hierarchical and charismatic gifts and adorns [Her] with His fruits (cf. Eph 4:11-12; 1 Cor 12:4; Gal 5:22)." Number 12 of the document goes on to treat the topic of charisms precisely in the context of the exercise of the priesthood:

> It is not only through the sacraments and the ministries of the Church that the Holy Spirit sanctifies and leads the people of God and enriches it with virtues, but, "allotting his gifts to everyone according as He wills" (1 Cor 12:11), He distributes special graces among the faithful of every rank. By these gifts He makes them fit and ready to undertake the various tasks and offices which contribute towards the

---

[41] Second Vatican Council, Constitution on the Liturgy, *Sacrosanctum Concilium*, no. 7; cf. *LG*, nos. 10-11.

renewal and building up of the Church, according to the words of the Apostle: "The manifestation of the Spirit is given to everyone for profit (1 Cor 12:7)."

Experience confirms, in fact, that where the filial priesthood of the baptized and the paternal priesthood of the ordained are lived out in profound, mutually respectful communion, the Holy Spirit is pleased to manifest Himself in all the gratuitous freedom characterizing His mode of personhood in Love, which He does precisely by communicating an abundance of charisms "for the common good." Prominent among such charisms are vocations to the consecrated life, which embody and adorn the Church-Bride and, in so doing, intensify Her missionary dynamism. The Spirit, then, does not merely inspire cordial, merciful, and fruitful relations of paternity and filiation between pastors and the lay faithful. In addition, He pours Himself freely into His multiple and various gifts, so as to manifest in His own way the Trinitarian glory of absolute, reciprocal, and fruitful Self-gift. In all its forms, the consecrated life is an essential testimony in the Church to this gratuity and fecundity of Trinitarian Love, which reawakens the Spirit of holiness among pastors and faithful while stimulating the missionary conversion of communities. In this sense, there is nothing surprising in the phenomenon of a charismatic Pope who promotes the evangelical counsels, "a poor Church for the poor," two synods on the family, a Jubilee of mercy, and so a new evangelization—all in continuity with his predecessors, even as he uses "new methods, a new ardor, and a new language." Blessed be God for having accompanied the Pentecost of the Second Vatican Council with such exceptional Pontiffs—true fathers who have given the papacy a moral and spiritual authority unique in the world today.

I think we may safely say, then, that the Trinitarian, Eucharistic, and nuptial ecclesiology initiated by the Second Vatican Council, which saw the Church as a "mystery of communion," is open to the pneumatological development sketched in the previous pages. As the foregoing account shows, the Church participates in the Trinitarian relations, not only in the intimacy of believers' souls, but also in Her own sacramental, hierarchical, and charismatic structures. The relation between the different states of life thus becomes a place in which the Church manifests the reciprocal and fruitful Love of the divine Persons who have involved themselves in our history.

An approach to the priesthood in terms of Trinitarian ecclesiology can help meet the need for a "spirituality of communion" that is relevant to all the states of life and is therefore fully rooted in the Church and Her mission. Nothing, in fact, does more to strengthen differentiated, well-ordered communion among the Church's various communities than the humble and grateful awareness that we all participate in the communion of the divine Persons, that we all share in the Love of the Father for the Son and the Love of the Son for the Father, as well as in the joy of the Spirit, Who glorifies Father and Son in and through the mutual love of creatures. It is this ultimate horizon, it seems to me, that finally justifies the difference in kind, and not merely in degree, between the two modes of participation in the one and only priesthood of Christ. For this difference is not a way of protecting the prerogatives of the clergy, but of ensuring that everyone, pastors and faithful of every charismatic stripe, vie in reciprocal love to advance the common pursuit of a Spirit-led service for the hope of the world.

In my humble opinion, Catholic theology of priesthood should continue this line of inquiry, which is a valuable resource for the pastoral and missionary conversion called for by Pope Francis.[42]

---

[42] The missionary conversion promoted by the Pope involves a re-discovery of the value of the parish as "the presence of the Church

Friends of the Bridegroom

The Church's renewed awareness of Her priestly character, in fact, would broaden horizons, reconcile differences, strengthen communion and, in consequence, motivate the far-ranging priestly renewal needed in a critical and ecumenical time like ours. On the account sketched here, we can retrieve and promote the full value of the common priesthood, without needing to fear any undue exaltation of one priesthood at the expense of the other. The whole point, after all, is just the opposite: The two modes of participation appear conjoined at the highest point and the highest level. Indeed, the two are correlative, and both are indispensable, just as both are ordered towards the Church's evangelizing and sacramental mission.

Conclusion

The foregoing, dear friends, is an exploratory essay that, inspired by the Second Vatican Council, draws on the doctrine of the Holy Spirit for deeper insight into priesthood in the Church. This pneumatological enrichment, it seems to me, has many implications for priestly spirituality, both lay and ministerial, for the relationship between pastors and faithful, for the joint pastoral and missionary responsibility of all the Church's members, for the communion of the states of life, the service of the poor, and the nurturing of vocations, and, above all, for the Church Herself as a mystery of communion at the service of the world's joy and hope.

In these remarks, I have shared with you convictions matured during twenty years' experience of priestly formation as a Sulpician. These convictions also represent the fruit both of my teaching and research as a professor of sacramental theology in Rome and of my responsibility for helping choose and accompany bishops at the

---

in a given territory," as a "community of communities, a sanctuary where the thirsty come to drink in the midst of their journey, and a center of constant missionary outreach." *Evangelii Gaudium*, no. 28.

service of the two most recent Popes, Benedict XVI and Francis. The present reflections make no claim to do anything more than offer testimony of theological insight conditioned by the ministries that I have exercised. Their sole aim is to contribute to the reform of the Church by means of a broad-ranging "priestly renewal for our time." This expression brings me back to my title, which I have chosen in honor of the acknowledgment offered to me with such grace and generosity today in this excellent institution of priestly formation. My thanks to you all.

Marc Cardinal Ouellet,
Prefect of the Roman Congregation for Bishops
Baltimore, November 15, 2016

Chapter 2

Priestly Celibacy and the Life of the Church: Contemporary Values and Challenges[43]

Peter said, "We have given up our possessions and followed you." He answered them, "Amen I say to you, there is no one who has given up house or wife or brothers or parents or children for the sake of the Kingdom of God who will not receive much more in this age and, in the world to come, eternal life."[44]

From all sides today, we hear a demand for the truth about priestly celibacy. This demand is made in the name of the personal development of priests, in the name of historical research,[45] and even in the name of justice. Cases of abandonment of the ministry because of the requirement of celibacy have long been known, and have generally been treated with a discretion that is not always interpreted

---

[43] Conference published in English: "Le célibat sacerdotal et la vie de l'Église," in *Celibacy and the Priesthood: Divine Gift and Cultural Anomaly*, edited by Arthur Kennedy (Boston: Saint Botolph Press, 2012), pp. 1-39.
[44] Lk 18:28-30.
[45] E. Abbot, *A History of Celibacy* (Da Capo Press, 2001).

benignly.[46] But in recent times, widely publicized scandals have forced the Church to a genuine examination of conscience and to a change of attitude with respect to society in general and especially with respect to the treatment of victims of sexual abuse and their offenders. The American bishops have exercised firm leadership in this regard, with the support of the Holy See, which has issued official apologies on several occasions.[47] These developments reveal a genuine search for reconciliation and justice, particularly with regard to victims of sexual abuse by clergy.[48]

In the pastoral sphere, the crisis of vocations and the dramatic situation of Christian communities in some areas provide additional reasons to question once again the appropriateness of upholding the universal requirement of celibacy for ordained ministers in the Latin Church. The new conditions in which priestly ministry must be exercised and which make it increasingly difficult to attain a celibacy that is fully developed and fulfilling, seriously affect the morale of priests, and doubtless their health[49] as well. This, of course, has an effect on the promotion of new vocations.

---

[46] D. Cozzens, *Sacred Silence: Denial and the Crisis in the Church* (Liturgical Press, 2002).

[47] We recall the encounter of Pope Benedict XVI with victims of abuse on April 17, 2008, during his apostolic journey to the United States; he made a similar gesture during World Youth Day in Sydney, Australia, on July 19, 2008; and, at the request of the Canadian bishops, he met with an official delegation of the Canadian First Nations in Rome on April 29, 2009, as a sign of compassion and solidarity during the "Truth and Reconciliation" Commission currently taking place in Canada.

[48] Since then, at the request of Pope Francis, the summit on "The Protection of Minors in the Church" was held in Rome from 21 to 24 February 2019, which resulted in the *Motu proprio Vos estis Lux Mundi* of May 7, 2019.

[49] Cf. D.R. Hoge, *The First Five Years of the Priesthood: A Study of Newly Ordained Catholic Priests* (Liturgical Press, 2002).

Moreover, powerful cultural forces openly assert their rejection of the Catholic sexual ethic as well as their contempt for the discipline of celibacy, since, according to "gender theory,"[50] the sexual difference is merely a cultural construct without foundation in a universal human nature.[51] We are far, here, from the biblical anthropology of the image of God that forms the basis of Western culture. The contemporary celibacy crisis is, therefore, not only a moral or spiritual crisis; it is also an anthropological crisis. It is fundamentally the result of the loss of a sense of nuptiality and fruitfulness, which goes hand in hand with the eclipse of God in the culture.

We, too, will attempt to articulate the truth about priestly celibacy. How do we evaluate the charism of celibacy today, and understand its relation to the priestly vocation? Contemporary cultural and pastoral challenges oblige us to a new examination of the reasons for priestly celibacy. We will not treat directly the relation between the celibacy of priests and cases of deviance and abuse, since the chief object of our study will be the formation of priests. We will, then, focus our attention on the biblical and patristic foundations for the importance of priestly celibacy, without losing sight of the question of whether it is opportune to uphold the universal requirement of celibacy for priests of the Latin Church. It is no longer enough, today, to repeat the ancient motivations to quiet the murmuring; above all, we must give back to priests and to candidates to the priesthood the enthusiasm that ought to radiate from the ministers of the Word of God. A new approach is proposed here to help accomplish the theological and pastoral

---

[50] J. Butler, *Gender Trouble: Feminism and the Subversion of Identity* (Routledge, 1990); T. Anatrella, *Le règne de Narcisse: Les enjeux du déni de la différence sexuelle* (Paris: La Renaissance, 2005).

[51] See Michel Boyancé, *Hommes, femmes, entre identités et différences* (Paris: Les Presses universitaires de l'IPC, 2013).

discernment appropriate to the times, and to offer some points of orientation for a renewal of priestly formation.

I. Is the ecclesiastical law of priestly celibacy still viable?

A. *The current crisis of credibility of the Church and Her ministers*

The question regarding priestly celibacy is particularly acute today, after the shock suffered by the Catholic Church in the United States with the explosion of the scandal of ephebophilia and pedophilia among members of the clergy in 2002. The price paid for this scandal far exceeded what anyone could have imagined. And I do not think first of the financial price — which was, in fact, astronomical — but rather of the vertiginous decline in credibility brought about by the revelations of the extent and duration of the crimes committed by priests on innocent victims.

The repercussions of this crisis extended far beyond the borders of the United States. They led to a strengthening of the judicial and disciplinary measures of the Roman Church regarding the abuses and the prevention of such acts, so totally contrary to the spirit of the Gospel. The widely used watchword "zero tolerance" responded correctly to the assault of the media, but it forms only the beginnings of a response to this moral tragedy that has profoundly damaged the credibility of the Catholic Church and Her ministers.

I propose not to analyze this crisis in detail,[52] but rather to indicate what direction a global response must take if it would restore confidence and self-respect not only to priests already exercising the ministry, but above all to those men on the path towards definitive commitment in priesthood. Let us acknowledge from the outset

[52] Cf. G. J. McGlone, "Prevalence and Incidence of Roman Catholic Clerical Sex Offenders," in *Sexual Addiction and Compulsivity* 10 (2003), pp. 111-121, posted on Taylor and Francis Online; D. R. Hoge; CCCB, *From Pain to Hope*: Report from the CCCB Ad Hoc Committee on Child Sexual Abuse, 1992; D. B. Cozzens.

that a decisive step in redressing the situation has been taken: The courage, humility, and sense of justice[53] shown by those who had to face this crisis directly suggest that priestly vocations will rise again and again.

We must add nonetheless that, in spite of the relative calm of the present moment, marked tensions remain in places of formation, in the relationship between priests and bishops, and in pastoral practice, which must guarantee an environment that is safe from all points of view. The morale of priests continues to suffer, and their pastoral dynamism betrays the effects of the new restrictions imposed on their behavioral code. Do not such conditions run the risk of increasing their solitude, decreasing their self-esteem, and driving them towards other forms of compensation?

B. The challenges of priestly life in contemporary culture

The moral crisis that had its epicenter in the archdiocese of Boston takes its place within the evolution of contemporary culture, marked as it is by secularization, the sexual revolution, and the liberalization of mores.[54] Hence a growing incomprehension in the face of priestly celibacy, and even the systematic attacks that we see in media on a grand scale.

The celibacy of the priest is not only suspected of hypocrisy and ridiculed; at times it is disgraced and denounced as a shameful masquerade. In the sphere of values, the reference to the Gospel that

---

[53] *Promise to Protect, Pledge to Heal: Charter for the Protection of Children and Young People, Essential Norms*, United States Conference of Catholic Bishops, revised June 2005.

[54] See Benedict XVI, "The Church and the Scandal of Sexual Abuse", French translation by S. Gallé, Catholic Documentation, April 11, 2019, https://www.la-croix.com/Urbi-et-Orbi/Documentation-catholique/Eglise-dans-le-Monde/LEglise-scandale-abus-sexuels-article-pape-emerite-Benoit-XVI-2019-04-16-1201016056.

is the basis for the life and the ministry of priests has been replaced by a prevailing cultural mind-set, which Benedict the XVI dared to call the "dictatorship of relativism."[55] Such an anthropocentric mentality not only adapts to the fact of religious pluralism, but adopts as a principle the idea that Christian truth is one opinion among many. To these cultural elements, we add the hedonism and the marketing of sex that pervades the digital world. In this context, the witness borne by celibate priests or even by consecrated persons generally appears as the value of another age, maybe, but one that no longer speaks to us today.

Even within the Church, notwithstanding repeated affirmations of the value of priestly celibacy, we note growing pressure to abolish its obligatory character, since we must respond to the pastoral needs of communities deprived of the celebration of the Eucharist because of a shortage of priests. In some circles, there is a lingering resentment for the Church's Magisterium, which made the definitive decision to reserve priestly ministry to men. This resentment gives rise to a passive resistance to the promotion of priestly vocations, which resembles a more or less silent protest. The general climate of communion that allows vocations to emerge is profoundly affected, and we run the danger of drifting towards non-Catholic models of the Church.

On the other hand, advances in exegesis and contemporary interpretation of the Scriptures have not yet yielded all their anticipated spiritual fruit. Thus far, the critical dimension of exegesis has prevailed over an emphasis on the spiritual significance of Christ's call to follow Him (*sequela Christi*). Furthermore, doubts often linger even in Catholic circles regarding the biblical foundations for

---

[55] See Cardinal Joseph Ratzinger, homily of the Mass before the Conclave, April 18, 2005: "Little by little a dictatorship of relativism is being built up which recognizes nothing as definitive and retains only its own ego and desires as its ultimate measure."

Mary's virginity, the affirmation of Christ's divinity, and the form of life of the Apostles who followed Christ. Consequently, there is a widening distance between the official teaching of the Church and a parallel academic "magisterium" that makes it difficult to unite the intellectual formation of candidates to the priesthood to the spiritual convictions essential for a definitive commitment in priestly celibacy.

C. Priesthood and celibacy: is it time to separate them?

A variety of factors from the spheres of history, culture, pastoral work, and ecumenism converge to compel the Church of today to a renewed reflection on the importance and the pertinence of maintaining the obligation of celibacy for priests in the future. Are we to sacrifice those communities that lack a priest to safeguard an ecclesiastical discipline that is respectable enough, but the value of which is not essential to the priesthood? Does not the Church's contemporary awareness of being grounded in the Eucharist raise a legitimate question as to whether we ought not to prefer access to the latter to upholding a law that is increasingly contested and hard to enforce? Would not the possibility of a choice offer a solution to the shortage of priestly vocations? At the point where we are in a world of rapid and global communication, could not the model of the Eastern Catholic Church be progressively expanded, all the while safeguarding a preference for vocations to celibacy?

These questions are asked with acuity and demand serious answers that are not content with a mere reaffirmation of traditional doctrine and discipline. We can imagine, of course, the colossal challenge involved in changing a two-thousand-year tradition and the very serious reasons that would have to justify it. The dissociation of the charisms of priesthood and celibacy in the Latin Church could not be justified simply by the existential difficulty priests have with living celibacy happily in the current context, since such a motivation would mean that we have forgotten the grace of God and resigned ourselves in the face of the task of evangelizing the culture. The profound impetus for this dissociation, if it were to take place, could only come from a spiritual discernment that resists cultural pressures and is exercised in the spirit of the universal Church. We must first take stock of the heritage of the tradition of ecclesiastical celibacy in order to assess its importance and fittingness. Only thus will we be able to articulate an adequate response to the challenges of today.

II. The tradition of ecclesiastical celibacy: its value and its challenges

A. *The essential message of the Church in the first centuries*

In order to appreciate the essential message of the Church of the first centuries on the subject of celibacy and clerical continence, we must keep in mind the Old Testament tradition, which exalts marriage and fruitfulness as the divine blessing *par excellence*. Contrary to the religious culture of Greece and even Rome, virginity does not belong to the values and institutions of the Old Testament.[56]

The emergence of the Christian ideal of virginity and ecclesiastical celibacy has its source entirely in the historical and eschatological novelty of Jesus Christ. Jesus' call to His disciples to follow Him implies "leaving everything,"[57] even marriage and family life, to be "with Him" and to be sent out "to preach."[58] In its newness and in its demands, the Apostles' form of life (*apostolica vivendi forma*) reflects the "new creation"[59] that comes into being from

[56] Cf. E. Abbot, pp. 21-54.
[57] Lk 14:26: cf. note 1 of TOB: "Unlike Mt 10:37, Lk mentions here the love of the bride who must also come after the love of Christ (cf. 18:29)"; Lk 18:29.
[58] Mk 3:14.
[59] Cf. 2 Cor 5:17.

the grace and the truth that have appeared in Jesus Christ. This form represents a radical testimony of faith and love in following Christ, "the firstborn of many brethren."[60] This apostolic form of life in communion with the Lord was to serve as a matrix for all the forms of consecration to come in the history of the Church. Even though it took time for this new lifestyle to emerge in the consciousness and the practice of the Church, from the outset, Jesus' personal call to His disciples inaugurated a radically new brotherhood, founded no longer on the ties of flesh and blood but on the Word of God received and put into practice in fraternal and Eucharistic communion.

The ecclesiastical tradition of celibacy and of the continence of clerics did not appear as a sudden novelty at the beginning of the fourth century, but as the confirmation in discipline, in the East as well as the West, of a tradition that can be traced back to the Apostles.[61] When the Council of Elvira in Spain in 306 stipulated that priests were obliged to live perfect continence, we must understand that this requirement of the Church in the first centuries included both celibacy and the prohibition of remarriage, and perfect continence for those who were already married.[62]

The profound motivation we find in this tradition does not depend first on the emergence of the Christian ideal of virginity,

---

[60] Rom 8:29.

[61] See Christian Cochini, *Les Origines apostoliques du célibat sacerdotal* (Paris: Le Sycomore, 1981); Henri Crouzel, "Le célibat et la continence ecclésiastique dans l'Église primitive: leurs motivations," in *Sacerdoce et célibat: Études historiques et théologiques*, edited by Joseph Coppens (Louvain Peeters, 1971), pp. 333-371.

[62] See C. Cochini, *Les Origines*, p. 65; Alfons-Maria Stickler, "L'évolution de la discipline du célibat dans l'Église en Occident de la fin du âge pratristique au conseil de Trente," in J. Coppens, op. cit, p. 373ff.; H. Crouzel, ibid.; Roger Gryson, *Les origines du célibat ecclésiastique, du 1er au septième siècle* (Gembloux: Duculot, 1970).

but rather on the exercise of the apostolic ministry itself. In fact, the motives for celibacy expressed by the Fathers refer to the service of the Word and to the ministry of prayer, both of which require on the part of the priest a testimony of purity that surpasses the perspective of Old Testament worship. For example, we read in the oft-cited decree of the Council of Carthage:

> It is fitting that the holy bishops and priests of God, as well as the Levites, i.e., those who are in the service of the divine sacraments, observe perfect continence, so that they may obtain in all simplicity what they are asking from God; what the apostles taught and what antiquity itself observed, let us also endeavor to keep.[63]

This decree played an important historical role in upholding the tradition of ecclesiastical celibacy, particularly in the Middle Ages and at the Council of Trent. It is not necessary, for our purposes, to delve further into the controversial debate about the apostolic origins of priestly celibacy.[64] It is enough to retain that the tradition of the first centuries justifies the perfect continence of clerics for reasons drawn, not first from the ideal of virginity, but from the exercise of the priestly ministry.

Saint Paul himself appears as an emblematic figure of perfect continence, whether he was unmarried or a widow.[65] Besides

---

[63] See the Council of Carthage of 390 (CC 149, p. 13), cited in C. Cochini, *Les Origines*, p. 25.

[64] Gustave Bickell and François-Xavier Funk resumed this controversy in Germany at the end of the nineteenth century. They were followed by Elphège-Florent Vacandard and Dom Henri Leclerc on the side of Funk, who contests the apostolic origin, and by A. M. Stickler and C. Cochini on Bickell's side, who says so. For Cochini's critique, see Roger Balducelli, *Theological studies* 43 (1982) pp. 693-705.

[65] L. Legrand, "Saint Paul et le célibat," in J. Coppens, op. cit., pp. 316ff.; Joachim Jeremias, "War Paulus Witwer?", in *Zeitschrift für*

advising his flock to be and to act as he[66] — that is, to remain free of carnal concupiscence — he recommends that Christian spouses abstain from conjugal relations for a time to dedicate themselves more liberally to prayer. If this is the case for spouses, we may conclude with the Fathers that it is that much more the case for the ministers of the Word and the Eucharist, who continually represent the people of God in prayer.[67]

Origen's Homily 6 on Leviticus, in which he comments on the prayer of Moses and Aaron for the people, is remarkable on this subject. He essentially expresses the conviction that the ministry of intercession accompanied by this witness obtains graces more simply and efficaciously for the people. As Cochini relates:

> Being permanently in God's presence, for the people he leads, the minister of the New Covenant does not have the leisure needed for married life, the freedom to be occupied with what would henceforth alienate his spiritual energies. Ephræm, Jerome, Ambrose, Siricius — all advocates of clerical continence — are only repeating, in different words, this leitmotiv borrowed from Scripture.[68]

This is also true of the ministry of preaching, which obtains its effect of conversion more easily when it is supported by the personal and institutional witness of the priest. As for the recommendation of Saint Paul to Timothy and Titus regarding the choice of candidates for bishop and deacon, "husband of one wife

---

neutestamentliche Wissenschaft und die Kunde der älteren Kirche, T. 25, Berlin, 1926, p. 310ff.

[66] Cf. 1 Cor 7:7.

[67] See Pope Siricius's decrees *Directa* and *Cum in unum* (C. Cochini, *Les Origines*, pp. 28-34).

[68] C. Cochini, *Les Origines*, p. 279.

only" (*Unius uxoris virum*),[69] the decretal *Cum in unum*, which played an important role both in the Synod of Rome in 386 and for Pope Siricius, developed an exegesis that sets aside the pursuit of conjugal life and establishes the choice of monogamous men, faithful to one woman, as a guarantee of future continence (*propter continentiam futuram*).[70]

The tradition of ecclesiastical celibacy at the origins of the Church has been the object of numerous studies and remains controversial. Whatever the nuances concerning its relation with the Old Testament and its ties to the surrounding pagan cultures, it nonetheless clearly affirms the novelty of the Christian priesthood and the new form of life it implies for the ministers of the New Covenant. These latter bear witness to the eschatological ministry of Jesus Christ through their radical commitment in following Him. According to the tradition of the Fathers, this commitment includes the practice of perfect continence even if the ministers are married:[71]

> If the scriptural texts themselves do not enable us to know what kind of lives the apostles led after their call, the Fathers, for their part, are unanimous in declaring that those who might have been married gave up their marital lives and practiced perfect continence.[72]

---

[69] Cf. 1 Tm 3:2-12.

[70] C. Cochini, *Les Origines*, p. 33, the same interpretation can be found in Saint Ambrose, Epiphany of Salamis, and the Ambrosiaster.

[71] As Clement of Alexandria, Tertullian, Isidore of Pelusa, Eusebius of Caesarea, the Ambrosiaster, and Saint Jerome attest. See C. Cochini, *Les Origines*, pp. 104ff.

[72] C. Cochini, *Les Origines*, p. 107. The author adds: "Their common feeling on this point constitutes an authorized hermeneutics of the Scripture texts in which reference is made to the detachment

B. *The Church's response to periodic questioning*

After the official adoption of Christianity in the Roman Empire, the Church enjoyed a period of freedom and rapid expansion, and the ecclesiastical discipline of celibacy had to be periodically reiterated. In the Middles Ages and especially in the Renaissance, this discipline became the object of controversy because of the general decline in mores and the scandals that embroiled all levels of the hierarchy. Due in large part to a system of revenues centered on benefices, this decadence placed the clergy too much in the way of interests that were either economic or of the private juridical order. Despite these counter-witnesses, the Church confirmed tradition and enacted reforms, with the help of holy reformers who were a source of spiritual renewal and missionary expansion. The profession of the evangelical counsels in various religious and monastic communities served as a stimulus, in spite of everything, to uphold the ideal of priestly celibacy even for the secular clergy. A. M. Stickler concludes his study of the Middle Ages in these terms:

> Despite the pressures often brought to bear even at the heart of the Church, she never questioned the foundation and the application of the law of celibacy, and never allowed herself to lose the essential: marriage after the reception of major orders was never tolerated; and the continuation of conjugal life was forbidden after ordination to candidates already married. Through the course of the ages, the discipline became even more severe. Marriages that major clerics claimed to have contracted were declared null, and the ordination of men already married was looked upon less and less favorably.[73]

practiced by the disciples of Christ, and in particular of Mt 19:27 and Luke 18:28-30."

[73] A. M. Stickler, loc. cit., p. 440.

Friends of the Bridegroom

The Council of Trent solemnly defended the value of celibacy against the opinion of the Reformation[74] and sanctioned its obligatory character for the clergy. This obligation was finally inserted into the *Code of Canon Law* of 1917.[75] The Church's concrete reform was due, above all, to the restoration of the ministry of the bishop, the creation of seminaries, and the spiritual renewal of the sixteenth and seventeenth centuries.

Vatican Council II approved and reconfirmed this legislation of the Church. Reaffirming the Church's traditional high esteem for this gift of God, the Council highlighted the various reasons celibacy is fitting for the priesthood:

> By preserving virginity or celibacy for the sake of the Kingdom of Heaven priests are consecrated in a new and excellent way to Christ. They more readily cling to him with undivided heart and dedicate themselves more freely in him and through him to the service of God and of men. They are less encumbered in their service of his kingdom and of the task of heavenly regeneration. In this way they become better fitted for a broader acceptance of fatherhood in Christ. By means of celibacy, then, priests profess before men their willingness to be dedicated with undivided loyalty to the task entrusted to them, namely, that of espousing the faithful to one husband and presenting them as a chaste virgin to Christ. They recall that mystical marriage, established by God and destined to be fully revealed in the future, by which the Church holds Christ as her only spouse. Moreover they are made a living sign of that world to come, already present through faith and charity, a world in which

[74] Session 24, canons 9-10.
[75] Can. 132, § 1.

the children of the resurrection shall neither marry, nor be given in marriage.[76]

The Council was very aware that there are many in the world today who declare perfect continence impossible: "So much the more humbly and perseveringly in union with the Church ought priests demand the grace of fidelity, which is never denied to those who ask" (ibid.).

Ten years later, Pope Paul VI, deeply aware of contemporary objections and the challenges of our time, took up once again the entire question of celibacy and developed the theological, spiritual, and pastoral motivations expressed succinctly by the Council.

Among the reasons motivating the Church's attitude, we call attention to the testimony rendered to the novelty of Christ:

> This is the mystery of the newness of Christ, of all that He is and stands for; it is the sum of the highest ideals of the Gospel and of the kingdom; it is a particular manifestation of grace, which springs from the Paschal Mystery of the Savior. This is what makes the choice of celibacy desirable and worthwhile to those called by our Lord Jesus. Thus they intend not only to participate in His priestly office, but also to share with Him His very condition of living.[77]

Pope Paul VI goes on to develop the ecclesiological reasons for priestly celibacy, stressing that "the priest takes on a closer likeness to Christ, even in the love with which the eternal Priest has loved the Church His Body and offered Himself entirely for her sake, in order to make her a glorious, holy and immaculate

---

[76] Second Vatican Council, *Presbyterorum Ordinis*, no. 16. Hereafter: PO.

[77] Saint Paul VI, Encyclical *Sacerdotalis Caelibatus*, no. 23. Hereafter: SC.

Spouse."[78] The new humanity thus born from the virginal and supernatural fruitfulness of Christ and the Church receives from the priest's witness a profound stimulus towards the charity and spiritual fruitfulness of its members. The Pope also refers to the eschatological meaning of celibacy, for "the pilgrim People of God are on a journey through the vicissitudes of this life towards their heavenly homeland, where the divine sonship of the redeemed will be fully revealed and where the transformed loveliness of the Spouse of the Lamb of God will shine completely."[79] This hope for our future heavenly inheritance is signified and already participated in here below, in the hearts of men and women consecrated to God for love of the Kingdom of Heaven.

Finally, the Holy Father dismisses the illusion of a "quick fix" for pastoral difficulties:

> We are not easily led to believe that the abolition of ecclesiastical celibacy would considerably increase the number of priestly vocations: the contemporary experience of those Churches and ecclesial communities which allow their ministers to marry seems to prove the contrary. The causes of the decrease in vocations to the priesthood are to be found elsewhere—for example, in the fact that individuals and families have lost their sense of God and of all that is holy, their esteem for the Church as the institution of salvation through faith and the sacraments. The problem must be examined at its real source.[80]

Hence his reaffirmation of the Church's legislation that he proclaimed from the outset:

[78] *Sacerdotalis Caelibatus*, no. 26.
[79] Ibid., no. 33.
[80] Ibid., no. 49.

We consider that the present law of celibacy should today continue to be linked to the ecclesiastical ministry. This law should support the minister in his exclusive, definitive and total choice of the unique and supreme love of Christ; it should uphold him in the entire dedication of himself to the public worship of God and to the service of the Church; it should distinguish his state of life both among the faithful and in the world at large.[81]

It goes without saying that in the postconciliar period, which was heavily influenced by a hermeneutic of discontinuity, the publication of the encyclical did not at all succeed in silencing dissent. The question came up again at the 1971 Synod on justice in the world and the ministerial priesthood, and again at the Synod on the formation of priests, which explicitly reaffirmed the Latin Church's tradition of reserving ordination to candidates who respond to the call of Christ to follow Him in priestly celibacy.[82]

C. *Contemporary perspectives on renewal*

Pope Benedict XVI places himself very consciously within the continuous ecclesial tradition of priestly celibacy, which he solemnly reaffirmed on the occasion of the publication of the apostolic exhortation *Sacramentum Caritatis*:

Celibacy is really a special way of conforming oneself to Christ's own way of life. This choice has first and foremost a nuptial meaning; it is a profound identification with the heart of Christ the Bridegroom who gives his life for his Bride. In continuity with the great ecclesial tradition, with

---

[81] Ibid., no. 14.
[82] See Saint John Paul II, Post-Synodal Apostolic Exhortation *Pastores Dabo Vobis*. Hereafter: *PDV*.

the Second Vatican Council and with my predecessors in the papacy, I reaffirm the beauty and the importance of a priestly life lived in celibacy as a sign expressing total and exclusive devotion to Christ, to the Church and to the Kingdom of God, and I therefore confirm that it remains obligatory in the Latin tradition. Priestly celibacy lived with maturity, joy and dedication is an immense blessing for the Church and for society itself.[83]

This confirmation takes up again the reflection that followed Paul VI's encyclical, and the declaration concerning the reservation of priestly ordination to men. We note here the emergence into the foreground of a nuptial symbolism in the line of developments in *Inter Insigniores, Mulieris Dignitatem*, and *Pastores Dabo Vobis*. This orientation is to be maintained in the future, since it also develops further and in greater depth the link between the Eucharist, the priesthood, and celibacy that we find in the encyclical *Ecclesia de Eucharistia*:

Could there ever be an adequate means of expressing the acceptance of that self-gift which the divine Bridegroom continually makes to his Bride, the Church, by bringing the Sacrifice offered once and for all on the Cross to successive generations of believers and thus becoming nourishment for all the faithful?[84]

An intense theological reflection on the priestly or presbyteral ministry both accompanied and followed the Magisterial

---

[83] Benedict XVI, Post-Synodal Apostolic Exhortation *Sacramentum Caritatis*, no. 24. Hereafter: SCa.

[84] Saint John Paul II, Encyclical *Ecclesia de Eucharistia*, no. 48. Hereafter: EdE.

interventions of the last decades.[85] The most promising and pertinent seems to me to be the line of thought of different authors who propose a deeper integration of the traditional motives for priestly celibacy, since even the encyclical *Sacerdotalis Caelibatus*, which confirms in the face of contemporary objections that ecclesiastical celibacy is well-founded, does not manage to go beyond a juxtaposition of different motives that lack a more profound principle of integration. Various authors have offered perspectives of renewal, concerning the Trinitarian dimension of the ministry,[86] the theology of vocation,[87] the eschatological dimension of the Eucharist,[88] the communitarian and fraternal dimension of the priesthood,[89] all within a profound vision of the sacramentality of the Church-communion.

The perspective we will develop here is a continuation of these attempts to integrate the profound reasons for priestly celibacy into an eschatological vision of the ministry, which presupposes a pneumatological Christology and a Trinitarian and nuptial ecclesiology. We hope to propose at least briefly a revival of priestly celibacy with the help of a theology of the Covenant and of fruitfulness.

---

[85] G. Martelet, *Deux mille ans d'Église en question. Théologie du Sacerdoce* (Cerf, 1984-1990), 3 vols.: vol. 1: *Crise de la foi, crise du prêtre*; vol. 2: *des Martyrs à l'Inquisition*; vol. 3: *du schisme d'Occident à Vatican II*.

[86] G. Greshake, *Priester Sein* (Herder, 1991), pp. 89ff.

[87] H. Urs von Balthasar, *Vocatione* (Rome: Editricerogate, 1966); *Christlicher Stand* (Freiburg i.Br.: Johannes Verlag Einsiedeln, 1997); P. Van Breemen, *Je t'aiappelépar ton nom* (Communio/Fayard, 1976).

[88] International Theological Commission (ITC), *The Priestly Ministry*, 1971, in *International Theological Commission: Texts and Documents 1969-1985* (San Francisco: Ignatius, 1989); P. Hacker, "Sacerdoce et eucharistie à l'heureprésente," in Coppens, op. cit., pp. 237-258.

[89] J. Esquerda Biffet, *Teologia de la Espiritualidad sacerdotal* (Madrid: BAC, 1976); M. Marini, *Le célibat sacerdotal* (Le forum, 2005).

III. Reviving priestly celibacy: On what conditions?

A. A deeper theological understanding of the ministerial priesthood

Our initial question regarding the viability of priestly celibacy led us to seek the profound meaning in a tradition that can be traced back to the ancient Church, and that has been affirmed through the centuries in the face of backsliding and decadence. The Latin Church finds Herself today at a crossroads. She must not only set off in the right direction but must do it for the right reasons.

If the fundamental problem we are facing has to do not only with the ministry and celibacy, but above all with faith in God, which "is disappearing from the cultural horizon of men,"[90] the response to this challenge cannot remain on the level of a pastoral reorganization according to the needs of communities that lack priests: it must confront the question of the value and the pertinence of ecclesiastical celibacy on the basis of the Word of God, and seek the reasons that would justify the uninterrupted continuity of the Latin tradition on this subject.

Paul VI's encyclical on celibacy gave a synthetic exposition of the Christological, ecclesiological, and eschatological motivations for priestly celibacy. While I acknowledge the remarkable quality

---

[90] See Benedict XVI, Letter to the Bishops of the Catholic Church, March 10, 2009: "In our time, when faith in vast regions of the world is in danger of being extinguished like a flame that can no longer be nourished, the predominant priority is to make God present in this world and to open access to God for men. Not to any god, but to that God who spoke on Sinai; to that God whose face we recognize in the love pushed to the end (cf. Jn 13:1)—in Jesus Christ crucified and risen. At this moment in our history, the real problem is that God disappears from the horizon of men and that while the light coming from God is extinguished, humanity lacks direction, and the destructive effects are increasingly manifested in its midst."

of this synthesis, it seems to me that the reasons offered in the encyclical could be articulated even more fully in a Trinitarian and nuptial perspective:

> In order to understand the ministry, we cannot take as our starting point Christ alone (the tendency of Western theology), nor the charismatic community as a work of the Spirit (the danger of the Reformation theologies of the ministry), but rather the Father who sends Christ and the Spirit in an inseparable unity to engender his people.[91]

The theological challenge of our day is to integrate the profound reasons for celibacy in a unified perspective that brings out what is specific to the priestly ministry. The key to this integration lies, in my opinion, in a deeper understanding of the relationship between the Eucharist and the Church as the wellspring of the great Eucharistic movement of this beginning of the millennium.[92] In the first millennium, the relation between the Eucharistic body of Christ and His ecclesial body was articulated vigorously upon the basis of the unity of the Church, thanks to a deeply realistic symbolic theology.[93] Beginning in the Middle Ages, the ecclesial dimension of the Eucharist grew less clear, giving way to an individualistic piety, the consequences of which led ultimately to the predominance of private Masses.

---

[91] G. Greshake, op. cit., p. 92.

[92] We are thinking here of the great Jubilee of the year 2000, which was intensely Eucharistic, the great Eucharistic documents (*Mane Nobiscum Domine, Ecclesia de Eucharistia, Sacramentum Caritatis, Redemptionis Sacramentum*, etc.), the Eucharistic year 2004-2005, the international Eucharistic Congresses of Guadalajara and Quebec, and finally the relaunch of Eucharistic adoration, etc.

[93] See Henri de Lubac, *Corpus mysticum: The Eucharist and the Church in the Middle Ages* (Paris: Aubier-Montaigne, 1944).

We must acknowledge, moreover, that if, at its origins, ecclesiastical celibacy conveyed a new breath of inspiration, this tradition also contained ambiguities rooted in the Levitical tradition and in philosophies of Platonic origin. We see these ambiguities, for example, in certain requirements for cultic purity and a suspicion of the flesh and of marriage that is widespread even among the Fathers.[94] The early Church had to defend the value of marriage against various Gnostic or Manichaean elements, all the while promoting perfect continence for clerics and the ideal of virginity for the Kingdom. The Levitical tradition is more familiar to us today, in its conception of the priesthood and in its requirements of ritual purity for cultic ministers. Furthermore, historical studies have allowed us to grasp better the positive thought of the Church face-to-face with the challenges of Platonism, and Gnostic and Manichaean sects. Much remains to be done, however, to reconcile the originality of the priesthood of the New Covenant and a certain continuity with the priesthood of the First Covenant.

I would dare to put forward the hypothesis that the horizon is now clear enough to allow us to reflect once again on the relationship between priesthood and celibacy, beginning from the Eucharistic mystery. We will do this here not in a purely ascetical and spiritual perspective, but in a sacramental and eschatological one that holds the key, in my opinion, to the profound integration of celibacy as a state of life at the heart of the exercise of the ministerial priesthood. Let us keep well in mind that, in the East as in the West, bishops maintained, without dispute and without interruption, the practice of perfect continence or celibacy; this fact invites us to continue our search for the deep theological reasons for this continuity.

[94] See Tertullian, *Exhortation to Chastity*, 9.

B. *Priesthood and celibacy: A new ministerial approach*

1. The Eucharistic mystery as an eschatological nuptial gift

At the Last Supper, on the night he was betrayed, our Savior instituted the eucharistic sacrifice of his Body and Blood. This he did in order to perpetuate the sacrifice of the Cross throughout the ages until he should come again, and so to entrust to his beloved spouse, the Church, a memorial of his death and resurrection: a sacrament of love, a sign of unity, a bond of charity, a paschal banquet in which Christ is consumed, the mind is filled with grace, and a pledge of future glory is given to us.[95]

Inspired by the liturgical reform of Vatican Council II, the Church has become more and more aware today of the eschatological dimension of the Eucharist.[96] Throughout history, She defended the doctrines of the Real Presence and of the Mass as sacrifice. In doing so, She was already defending the eschatological dimension of the Eucharist, that is to say, as the Apostolic Exhortation *Sacramentum Caritatis* puts it, the presence of the Paschal Mystery of Christ in the sacrament: "For us, the eucharistic banquet is a real foretaste of the final banquet foretold by the prophets (cf. Is 25:6-9) and described in the New Testament as 'the marriage-feast of the Lamb' (Rev 19:7-9), to be celebrated in the joy of the communion of saints."[97]

This eschatological sense of the Church's Eucharistic faith has its roots in the New Testament itself, as the following passages, for example, bear witness:

---

[95] Second Vatican Council, Constitution on the Sacred Liturgy *Sacrosanctum Concilium*, no. 47. Hereafter: SC.

[96] Cf. *EdE*, nos. 18-20; SCa, nos. 30-33.

[97] SCa, no. 31.

I say unto you, I will not drink again of the fruit of the vine until the day when I drink it again with you in the Kingdom of my Father.[98]

When I have been lifted up, I will draw all men to myself.[99]

He who eats my flesh and drinks my blood has eternal life, and I will raise him up on the last day.[100]

For each time that you eat this bread and drink this cup, you proclaim the death of the Lord until he comes.[101]

Let us rejoice and be glad, and give him glory, for behold the wedding feast of the Lamb![102]

These texts draw our attention to the mystery of the Trinity and the mystery of the Church, which meet in the priestly offering Christ makes of Himself to the Father in love, in the power of the Holy Spirit.[103] This sacrificial offering is given to the Church-Bride as a perpetual memorial of the New Covenant.

By the power of his Word and of the epiclesis pronounced over the Eucharistic species, the living Christ, whose death we announce until he comes, unites himself to the ecclesial community as to his Body and Bride. He transforms the offering of the assembled community into his own body and gives them in communion his Eucharistic body as a nuptial gift.[104]

[98] Mt 26:29.
[99] Jn 12:32.
[100] Jn 6:54.
[101] 1 Cor 11:26.
[102] Rev 19:7.
[103] Heb 9:14.
[104] *The Eucharist, God's Gift for the Life of the World*, Proceedings of the 49th International Eucharistic Congress, Quebec, Canada, 2008, CBAC, p. 39; for further developments, cf. Marc Ouellet, "The

This eschatological and nuptial gift of Christ the Lord to His Bride passes through the hearts and hands of His ministers, who exercise not only a sacramental office but, properly speaking, an eschatological service. This is what we must seek to understand more deeply in order to unify the Christological, ecclesiological, and eschatological reasons for priestly celibacy.

2. THE MINISTERIAL PRIESTHOOD AS ESCHATOLOGICAL SERVICE

Our exposition will not be complete until we have systematically integrated, along with the renewal of Eucharistic ecclesiology, the remarkable development in recent Magisterial texts of a theology of the priesthood as a representation of Christ the Bridegroom, in the context of a nuptial ecclesiology.[105] This development not only responds to the feminist demand for women to be admitted to ordained ministry;[106] it also signals a decisive step in the deeper understanding of the relationship between the Eucharist and the Church as mystery and ministry of the New Covenant. The conciliar renewal of the ministry of bishop, priest, and deacon seems to us to have prepared the way for such a deeper understanding.

Eucharist, a Bridal Gift," *Communio*, no. 149 (May-June 2000), pp. 19-40.

[105] See *PO*, no. 16; Saint John Paul II, Apostolic Letter *Mulieris Dignitatem*, no. 26 (hereafter: *MD*); *PDV*, no. 22; *CEC*, no. 1627; Apostolic exhortation *Vita Consecrata*, no. 34; *EdE*, no. 48; *SCa*, nos. 14, 27.

[106] *MD*, no. 26: "In the Eucharist is expressed above all sacramentally the redemptive act of Christ the Bridegroom towards the Bride Church. This becomes transparent and unequivocal when the sacramental service of the Eucharist, where the priest acts *"in persona Christi"*, is accomplished by man. This is an explanation that confirms the teaching of the Inter-Insigniore Declaration, published on the mandate of Paul VI to answer the questions raised by the question of the admission of women to the ministerial priesthood."

In fact, Vatican Council II presented the doctrine of the priesthood by taking as its starting point the service of the Word of God: "The People of God is formed into one in the first place by the Word of the living God, which is quite rightly sought from the mouth of priests."[107] This ministry of the Word is exercised in various ways, according to need and charisms, and is indispensable for the celebration of the sacraments. In the context of the celebration of the Eucharist, it attains its properly eschatological dimension, for here, "there is an inseparable union of the proclamation of the Lord's death and resurrection, the response of its hearers and the offering itself by which Christ confirmed the new covenant in his blood. In this offering the faithful share both by their sacrificial sentiments and by the reception of the sacrament."[108]

"The dilemma, word or Eucharist, must … be overcome," as the members of the International Theological Commission affirm. "It can be overcome by defining, as we have done, the priestly ministry as the service of the active, properly eschatological power of the Word of God — Jesus Christ who died and rose again — of which the visible signs are the announcement of the Gospel message and the sacramental actions."[109]

We can say, then, that the priest, minister of the Word, represents Christ the Bridegroom as God's definitive Word to humanity; this Word culminates in the Eucharist, the supreme act of sacrificial offering on the part of the High Priest of the New Covenant. This act of the divine Bridegroom is absolutely Trinitarian, for it implies the three divine Persons in the unity of Love that transcends time. This Love gives itself to us so that we might participate in it sacramentally, through the priest ordained for this purpose. Since

[107] PO, no. 4.
[108] Ibid.
[109] ITC, op. cit. at 89. The authors refer to Karl Rahner, "The Essence of the Ministerial Priesthood," in *Concilium* 43, p. 81.

he is sacramentally united to Christ the Bridegroom, the priest communicates in Him not only as a member of the ecclesial community, but first as a minister of Christ Himself, Who gives Himself bodily and virginally to His Bride, the Church.

It is by virtue of this ministerial service of the Paschal Mystery, which makes the Kingdom come even now, that priestly celibacy appears in all its splendor and sacramental coherence. Here, the ideal of perfect continence no longer appears as an ascetical requirement of cultic purity, but rather as an eschatological state of life in perfect harmony with the mystery celebrated. In other words, it is the irruption of the eschatological Kingdom in the Eucharistic mystery, nuptially uniting Christ and the Church, which fundamentally justifies the requirement of the Latin Church with respect to Her ministers and the pertinence of Her two-thousand-year tradition. Henri Crouzel summarizes the message of the Church's first centuries that inspires us here:

> Among the motivations that led to the imposition of celibacy or continence on clerics in the first centuries, the teaching of St. Paul and the gospels plays a role that is far from exclusive, but that remains essential: it is not only an extrinsic justification. Its eschatological dimension does not lie merely in the realization of a mythical or desirable immanence of the end of the world. The Kingdom of Heaven is underway from the moment of the Incarnation, and the time of the Church, if we may speak thus, is the time of an eschatology in becoming.[110]

It is good and desirable for the Eastern tradition to retain its freedom in the choice between marriage and celibacy, for the presence of married priests bears witness that the conjugal relation is

[110] H. Crouzel, loc. cit., p. 367.

not of itself soiled by a congenital impurity[111] that would render
the minister unworthy to celebrate the holy mysteries.[112] But it is
also good and desirable for the Latin tradition to retain its freedom
to unite the charism of celibacy with the exercise of the priestly
ministry, since this two-thousand-year tradition renders eloquent
testimony to the eschatological character of the Eucharist and of the
ministry. It is, at bottom, love and participation in the Kingdom-
in-becoming that justifies the call to live and to love as Christ
the Bridegroom. Behind the historical reasons — at times more
or less debatable — bearing on legal or moral purity formulated by
the witnesses of the ancient Church, it is the mission of serving
on the front lines of the coming of the Kingdom that seems to me
to be the final motivation for the Church's unfailing attachment
to this ecclesiastical discipline. In a word, this law is a homage of
faith and love that the Bride offers to Him Who is Her desire and
Her reason for being.

3. The spiritual fruitfulness of celibacy and priestly fraternity

This basic vision becomes even clearer when we turn our attention to the Trinitarian foundation of priestly ministry and to its
communitarian dimension. One of the major advances of Vatican
Council II was to stress episcopal collegiality and the sacramental

---

[111] See the decree *Dominus Inter*, from the Roman Synod to the Gallic
bishops, at the end of the fourth century or at the beginning of the
fifth, third canon, which reflects this negative vision of conjugal
trade. These prejudices are now overcome and no longer play a
role in the Church's motivation. After all, did Christ not elevate
marriage to the dignity of a sacrament and sanctify conjugal love?

[112] For example, Alexander Schmemann's life and theology honor
the oriental tradition of married priests. See *The Journals of Father
Alexander Schmemann 1973-1983* (Saint Vladimir's Seminary Press,
2000); *The Eucharist, Sacrament of the Kingdom* (Saint Vladimir's
Seminary Press, 1988).

fraternity of priests as intrinsic components of the Sacrament of Orders.[113]

Along the same lines, the Apostolic Exhortation *Pastores Gregis*, on the vocation of the bishop, makes explicit the Trinitarian foundation for the relational ontology that underlies the episcopal and presbyteral ministries:

> Christ's life is Trinitarian. He is the eternal and only-begotten Son of the Father and the anointed of the Holy Spirit, sent into the world; it is he who, together with the Father, pours out the Spirit upon the Church. This Trinitarian dimension, manifested in every aspect of Christ's life and activity, also shapes the life and activity of the Bishop.[114]

From the moment of his consecration, the bishop receives the fullness of the priesthood by being incorporated into the college of bishops; through the laying on of hands of the bishop, the priest, for his part, is made a cooperator of the episcopal order and a member of a college of priests. Following this sacramental logic, bishops exercise their ministry in an affective and effective solidarity that testifies to their hierarchical communion and their membership in the college of bishops.[115] This hierarchical and communitarian witness is essential to the life of the communion that is the Church. It forms a supporting structure rooted in the communion of the Trinity, inasmuch as the episcopal and presbyteral ministers incarnate the eschatological ministry of Christ and are ordained by the Spirit for the service of the common priesthood of the faithful.

---

[113] *LG*, no. 28; Decree *Christum Dominus* on the Pastoral Office of Bishops, no. 4; *PO*, no. 8.

[114] Saint John Paul II, Post-Synodal Apostolic Exhortation *Pastores Gregis*, no. 7.

[115] *Pastores Gregis*, no. 8.

In this collegial context of the fullness of the priesthood, ecclesiastical celibacy, maintained by the Church in both East and West, shows itself to be in perfect harmony with the spiritual fatherhood of the bishop, who points simultaneously to his Trinitarian origin and to the Eucharistic fruitfulness of the risen Christ. Ultimately, this fatherhood reveals the mystery of the Father, of whom the bishop is a privileged image, according to St. Ignatius of Antioch.[116]

a. The spiritual fatherhood of the bishop and of priests

The tradition which sees the Bishop as an image of God the Father is quite ancient. As Saint Ignatius of Antioch wrote, the Father is like an invisible Bishop, the Bishop of all. Every Bishop, therefore, stands in the place of the Father of Jesus Christ in such a way that, precisely because of this representation, he is to be revered by all. Consonant with this symbolism, the Bishop's chair, which especially in the tradition of the Eastern Churches evokes God's paternal authority, can only be occupied by the Bishop. This same symbolism is the source of every Bishop's duty to lead the holy people of God as a devoted father and to guide them — together with his priests, his co-workers in the episcopal ministry, and with his deacons — in the way of salvation. Conversely, as an ancient text exhorts, the faithful are to love their Bishops who are, after God, their fathers and mothers.[117]

This spiritual horizon of the bishop's fatherhood confers upon the witness of celibacy a dimension of fruitfulness that transcends

[116] See Saint Ignatius of Antioch, *Aux Magnésiens* 6, 1 (*PG*, 5, 764, *Sources chrétiennes* 10 [Paris, éd. du Cerf, 1969], p. 85); *Aux Tralliens* 3, 1 (*PG* 5, 780, ibid., p. 97); *Aux Smyrniotes* 8, 1 (*PG* 5, 852, ibid., p. 139).
[117] *Pastores Gregis*, no. 7.

reasons of pastoral availability, even if these retain all their importance. Celibacy lived out authentically, within the service of the ecclesial communion and in continuity with the Apostles' form of life (*apostolica vivendi forma*), represents for the Church an irreplaceable value, even if particular circumstances might justify different practices.[118]

As for priests, their service of ecclesial communion is rendered more fruitful by a celibacy taken up freely, which makes them "better fitted for a broader acceptance of fatherhood in Christ. By means of celibacy, then, priests profess before men their willingness to be dedicated with undivided loyalty to the task entrusted to them, namely that of espousing the faithful to one husband and presenting them as a chaste virgin to Christ (cf. 2 Cor.11, 2)."[119]

For the bishop, just as much as for priests, spiritual fatherhood goes hand in hand with the witness of sacramental fraternity, which makes the collegial and communitarian nature of the episcopate and the presbyterate concrete in personal and organic relations. All these bonds woven through the activity of the ministry testify to the triune love that gives itself to be shared, in and through the life of the Church at the heart of the world.

b. The pastoral charity of ministers and nuptial symbolism

The decree on the ministry and life of priests defines the ideal of priestly perfection from the life of the Good Shepherd. Priests exercise His "pastoral charity," which brings their life and their action into unity.[120] This pastoral charity flows above all from the Eucharistic sacrifice, which is "the root and center of the whole life

[118] For example, in some cases of conversion of married ministers from other Christian denominations.
[119] PO, no. 16.
[120] PO, no. 14.

of a priest. What takes place on the altar of sacrifice, the priestly heart must make his own."[121]

Pope John Paul II defined the love of Christ the Redeemer as a merciful love but also as a spousal love that therefore hopes for a response from redeemed humanity.[122] This vision takes its inspiration from a Johannine Christology and symbolic ecclesiology, which sees Jesus as the Bridegroom of humanity and John the Baptist, His prophet, as the "friend of the Bridegroom."[123] The "beloved disciple" also sees a strict relation between the scene at Cana, which is the first of Jesus' messianic signs, and the Hour of the Cross, which is already the celebration of the eschatological wedding feast of the Lamb. The Mother of Jesus occupies a central place in this event of the redemption, which Saint Irenaeus describes as the mystery of the "New Eve," associated with the "New Adam" in order to give birth to a new humanity.[124]

This nuptial symbolism, of biblical and patristic inspiration and based on the fundamental category of the Covenant, emerges with ever greater clarity in recent texts of the Church's Magisterium. The Church thus takes up again, on the far side of modern rationalism, the spiritual exegesis of the Word of God that gave the Fathers of the Church and the Middle Ages a rich tradition of symbolic and nuptial theology.[125] We recall here the text of *Pastores Dabo Vobis*, which applies this nuptial symbolism to the testimony of celibacy:

[121] PO, no. 14.
[122] Saint John Paul II, "Man and Woman He Created Them," in *Theology of the Body*, trans. Michael Waldstein (Boston: Pauline Books and Media, 2006).
[123] Jn 3:29.
[124] Saint Irenaeus, *Against Heresies*, III, 2, 3, *Christian Sources* 34 (Paris, ed. of the Deer, 1952).
[125] M. Ouellet, "Restoring the Word of God to Its Full Place: Introductory Report of Cardinal Marc Ouellet, General Rapporteur of the Synod," *La Documentation catholique*, no. 2411, November 2, 2008.

The Church, as the spouse of Jesus Christ, wishes to be loved by the priest in the total and exclusive manner in which Jesus Christ her head and spouse loved her. Priestly celibacy, then, is the gift of self in and with Christ to his Church and expresses the priest's service to the Church in and with the Lord.[126]

c. Ecclesiastical celibacy: a call for today

The eschatological event of Jesus Christ, Prophet and Founder of the Kingdom; the Apostles' form of life; the firm and progressive imposition of the law of ecclesiastical celibacy in the face of decadence and periodic contention; the conciliar and postconciliar reconfirmation of this gift and legislation; and the search for a deeper understanding of the theological reasons for this choice lead us to the following conclusion: The Church never linked priesthood and celibacy on the level of dogma, but She always maintained Her judgment on the pastoral value of the bond between the two, which expresses in the minister the "exclusive, definitive and total choice of the unique and supreme love of Christ."[127] Pope Benedict XVI, joining John Paul II, adds, "This choice has first and foremost a nuptial meaning; it is a profound identification with the heart of Christ the Bridegroom who gives his life for his Bride."[128] In consequence, Benedict XVI confirms once more the Church's will to maintain the obligatory character of ecclesiastical celibacy for the Latin Church.

This impressive continuity of the Church's pastoral judgment testifies to a discernment carried out in the light of the Holy Spirit, whose primary mission is to impress the form of Christ upon the

[126]*PDV*, no. 29.
[127]*SC*, no. 14.
[128]*SCa*, no. 24.

baptized and upon the missionaries of the Gospel. The identity crisis afflicting the priestly ministry, which we mentioned in opening, also entails a crisis of the value of celibacy. At the roots of this crisis is a failure to recognize both the call of God in Christ and the total availability demanded of the one chosen, who is to give himself to God without conditions and allow himself to be sent as a worker into the vineyard in the service of the ecclesial community.[129] Hans Urs von Balthasar remarked that, in our day, there is a tendency to water down the concept of vocation; we have lost sight of its biblical origins and its essential characteristics.[130] The latter appear in the Apostles' form of life (*apostolica vivendi forma*), which implies leaving "everything," even conjugal and family life, to follow Jesus in His witness to absolute love and His eschatological ministry of salvation.

This evangelical form of life corresponds to the Eucharistic commitment of the Lord, Who, for love, handed over His body once and for all to the extreme of sacramental distribution. He requires of the one He calls a response of the same order — that is, total, irrevocable, and without conditions. In this vocation to love, which bears witness to a new form of nuptiality and fruitfulness, the Lord expresses His own virginal and Eucharistic fruitfulness, to the praise of the glory of the Father and for the salvation of mankind. "It is the glory of my Father that you bear much fruit."[131] "Remain in me, as I in you, for without me you can do nothing."[132]

The Apostles' form of life continues in history in the forms of consecrated life, including the profession of the evangelical counsels of poverty, chastity, and obedience. These forms actualize

[129] H. Urs von Balthasar, "*Berufung*", in *Die antwort des Glaubens*, 2005, pp. 177-203.
[130] Ibid.
[131] Jn 15:8.
[132] Jn 15:5.

the fundamental biblical idea of vocation and appear in perfect harmony with the priestly ministry as eschatological service at the heart of the ecclesial community. While the profound motivation for consecrated virginity springs from the heart of the Bride, Who answers Her divine Bridegroom, the specific motivation for priestly celibacy emanates from the ministerial participation in the personal self-gift of the Bridegroom.

We could, of course, conceive that even for the Latin Church, another form of life, marriage, might be associated with pastoral ministry by virtue of an authentic "charism," which would, however, not include to the same degree the original experience of vocation in the biblical and New Testament sense.[133] This distinction between "vocation" in the strict sense and ecclesial "charism" can describe to some extent the difference between the Eastern and Latin traditions. The final judgment regarding this possibility belongs to the universal Church, which has thus far preferred, for serious reasons, to uphold as well-founded the law of obligatory ecclesiastical celibacy.

> The minister who, by concretely living his celibacy in love, joy, and hope, explicitly and actually refers his life to Christ, gives credibility to the Gospel, which he announces as a total and definitive value, a value of grace that transcends time. His life authenticates with a seal his announcement of the word of God.[134]

> Combining word and action, [the celibate] is the supreme sign of the presence of God and at the same time a living "contestation" of a world that is closed in on itself and thus is condemned to a spiritual asphyxiation: though called to

---

[133] H. Urs von Balthasar, *Berufung*, loc. cit., p. 193.
[134] ITC, op. cit., p. 104.

the fullness of the Infinite, it has opted for the finite as its all-sufficient end. This is why celibacy, like the Gospel, the Faith, and the Church, will always remain a scandal and a stumbling block for those who do not live the obedience in spirit to the mystery of Christ.[135]

At the end of this essay in discernment, we see with greater clarity that the Church cannot renounce the symbolic, sacramental, eschatological, and pastoral value of ecclesiastical celibacy. Despite mishaps and controversy, it remains a valid form of spiritual fatherhood that testifies to the Eucharistic fruitfulness of the Lord and His Bride. Our attempt at discernment follows in the footsteps of Paul VI's encyclical, while also indicating a path towards a deeper theological understanding of the relationship between celibacy and the priesthood.

What concrete implications can we draw from this vision for the initial and permanent formation of priests, in the dramatic circumstances we described at the outset? We will only touch upon a few aspects of this question, since a thorough treatment of it would require a conference of its own.

C. *Contemporary challenges in priestly formation*

1. Promoting a unified vision of the priestly ministry

In our day, marked as it is by a crisis of priestly identity that doubles as an intensification of the crisis of the credibility of ecclesiastical celibacy, the Church cannot revive priestly celibacy without offering something more than a reaffirmation of its worth and a strengthening of Her discipline.

The integration we attempted of all the traditional motivations for priestly celibacy in a Trinitarian, eschatological, and nuptial

[135] Ibid., p. 107.

vision of the priestly ministry, within the comprehensive horizon of a Eucharistic ecclesiology, seems to me to offer a valid alternative to the lack of vision that hinders new vocations and dulls enthusiasm in the formation of priests.

For, beyond pastoral reorganization and the contributions of the human sciences, it is enthusiasm for a faith-vision of the mystery of the priesthood that can, even today, move young people to commit themselves, in the face of all the opposing trends, in a daring, radical, and definitive response to the call of Christ.

The life and the ministry of priests reveal their eschatological value to the extent to which they affirm the transcendence of Jesus Christ through their disinterested service of the communion that is the Church. Through their ministry and lifestyle, priests participate in the eschatological love of Jesus. Their enthusiasm is obviously nourished by prayer and fidelity. Nevertheless, a Christological vision of the last things is often lacking, which would breathe new life into the preaching of the Kingdom and reveal the eschatological and ecclesial meaning of the Eucharistic mystery. In other words, priests must be indwelt by the splendor of Trinitarian Love. This indwelling comes to pass at the heart of the community as the Kingdom-in-becoming. Such a theological and pastoral vision could revive a sense for the gift of self and, consequently, for the pertinence of priestly celibacy.

2. Signposts and criteria for formation in priestly celibacy[136]

It is not by capitualating in the face of controversy or lamentation, nor by easing the requirements of priestly formation that we will stir up new vocations and motivate priests to engage their contemporaries. The holiness of a St. John Vianney depends in

---

[136] The Company of Saint-Sulpice, *For the Sake of the Kingdom: A Sulpician Approach to Formation in Priestly Celibacy.*

large measure on the faith-vision that upheld his personal, total, definitive, and fruitful response to the love of Christ. In other words, it is the awareness of a personal call of love, upheld by grace, that is the first condition for succeeding in the overcoming of self demanded by priestly celibacy. We can multiply human and technological resources all we like, but if there are lingering doubts about the value of ministry and of celibacy, priestly formation will fail to kindle the sacred zeal that burns in holy priests.

In this perspective, it is not by adding to a seminarian's already overburdened curriculum that we will overcome the current crisis. It is rather by ensuring that the vision of faith underlying the Catholic conception of the priesthood is appropriated and translated into a lifestyle that conforms to the eschatological ministry of Jesus. For example, formators would be well advised to ask themselves whether their program of formation, and especially entry into formation, marks with enough clarity and force a change in the seminarian's lifestyle and his commitment to following Christ. The responsibility of the bishop is primordial in this regard and presupposes a constant vigilance over the quality of spiritual and intellectual formation, as well as sustained personal contact with formators and the seminary community, so as to cultivate the fraternal relations that correspond to the collegial nature of priestly ministry.

That being said, the particular challenges of our time deserve special attention and adequate criteria for discernment. First of all, a reaffirmation of the value of priestly celibacy presupposes that the importance of marriage and the family is recognized. Candidates for the priesthood must be educated in a lifestyle that is properly priestly, and which testifies to an authentic affective maturity. To this end, formation should encourage the development of sacramental fraternity and friendships among priests. Moreover, the conditions of the ministry today include a close collaboration with laypeople engaged either in their secular responsibilities or in apostolic activities, or with pastoral ministers. This collaboration requires an openness to shared responsibility with the laity, as well as discernment and development of the charisms the Spirit stirs up among them for the good of the community.

The hypersexualization of Western culture requires, moreover, careful attention in the discernment of vocations, particularly with regard to the psychosexual identity of candidates, their capacities to relate to others, and their aptitude for the interior life and for the concrete practice of charity. The problem of homosexuality and its implications for formation in celibacy will be the object of an examination that is both rigorous and respectful of persons, in the spirit of the precise guidelines of the Holy See in this matter.[137]

On the level of spiritual formation, it would be fitting periodically to verify a candidate's willingness to leave everything and follow Christ generously and without conditions, even through trials and renunciations. Although diocesan priests do not profess the evangelical counsels, these remain a fundamental criteria for the authenticity of a response to Christ.

Since time is limited during the seminary years to develop all the dimensions of priestly formation, seminarians must be educated from the outset towards a mind-set of permanent formation, articulated around the candidate's personal responsibility and the coherence of his choices, with a view to a firm commitment to ongoing formation once he is ordained. The example of priests in

[137]Cf. Congregation for Catholic Education, *Instruction Concerning the Criteria for the Discernment of Vocations with regard to Persons with Homosexual Tendencies in View of Their Admission to the Seminary and to Holy Orders*, November 4, 2005; *Guidelines for the Use of Psychology in the Admission and Formation of Candidates for the Priesthood*, June 28, 2008.

ministry and the common activities of the diocesan presbyterate should serve to inculcate this mind-set.

Lastly, if the tightening of the behavioral code that governs human relations in the pastoral framework has proved to be necessary in the current circumstances, these restrictions ought nevertheless to leave room for trust and for the spontaneity of warm fraternal relationships in the context of an integral respect for persons and of the joy that radiates from an authentic Christian life.

Conclusion

Rather than seeking quick solutions for today's challenges, we chose to deepen our understanding of the reasons for the uninterrupted tradition of ecclesiastical celibacy. With the support of a theology of the Covenant rooted in the biblical symbolism of the wedding feast, and relying on a Christological renewal of eschatology, we envisaged priestly ministry and celibacy as an eschatological service of the Word of God that extends to the sacramental proclamation of the Paschal Mystery. That is to say, this service extends to the holy Eucharist, the nuptial mystery *par excellence* of Christ and the Church.

Our survey of the tradition, from the Apostles' form of life to the law of ecclesiastical celibacy, supported by serious contemporary studies, revealed a remarkable continuity in the perception of the affinities between the priestly ministry, the continence of married clerics, and celibacy. Despite some questionable ancient justifications for celibacy, and in the face of contestations and periods of decadence, the Church always maintained Her preference for the perfect continence of Her ministers, be they married or celibate. The example of the bishop in both the Eastern and Western traditions testifies to this. While we acknowledge the value of the Eastern Catholic tradition, which retains the choice between a celibate and a married clergy, does not the Latin tradition have the responsibility to renew itself, in fidelity to its own values, rather than borrowing from elsewhere short-term solutions to respond to its pastoral needs?

In conclusion, we can also ask ourselves in what concrete ways this vision can revitalize priestly celibacy. Is it realistic and operational enough to respond to the challenges facing the ministry and celibacy in our day? First of all, we will say that the perspective we have developed places in relief the eschatological significance of Jesus' existence, preaching, and Paschal Mystery. Such an approach restores the mystery of the priesthood to its rightful place at the heart of a Trinitarian and Eucharistic ecclesiology. It has more of a chance of kindling receptivity to the call of Christ and enthusiasm for a total and definitive gift of self. In spite of the challenges of celibacy and a contemporary situation that makes it harder to live a balanced affective life, young people today remain sensitive and open to a great ideal that gives meaning to their lives. Should not seminary formation bank on this capital of nobility and generosity?

As for the urgent pastoral needs that justify, for some, a by-now programmatic dissociation of celibacy from the priesthood, should we not confront these challenges with a vast new evangelization that would revitalize the faith, rather than demand married priests and women priests to fill vacant posts in affected communities? Revitalizing the faith through kerygmatic preaching and a renewed witness would be more fruitful in the long term than a rapid reorganization of communities with a view to solutions that would bring other problems in their wake. The Church's ecumenical experience is instructive in this regard and invites us to prudence rather than to questionable imitations.

The Church lives from the Eucharist, and communities have to be able to nourish themselves from it as often as possible. May they mobilize in listening to the Word of God, Eucharistic adoration, formation in the Christian life, the testimony of conjugal fidelity, and prayer for vocations, and God will hear and answer the Church's desire to be loved by priests who are holy witnesses of Christ the Bridegroom.

The questions and the tensions that traverse the Church at this beginning of the millennium point us finally to the Gospel and to the discussion of Jesus' contemporaries about His identity: "Who do the crowds say that I am?... And you, what do you say? *For you, who am I?*"[138]

Isn't the question addressed to the Church by the current crisis the same one Jesus once asked His disciples when the crowds began to leave Him: "Do you also want to go away?"[139] Simon Peter spoke and answered, "Lord, to whom should we go? You have the words of everlasting life."[140]

[138] Lk 9:18-20.
[139] Jn 6:67.
[140] Jn 6:68.

Chapter 3

Fiftieth Anniversary of *Presbyterorum Ordinis*

Presbyterorum Ordinis: A prophetic text for today[141]

Since the baptism of Clovis, the kingdom of Saint Louis, and the passion of Joan of Arc, many eminent figures of holiness have embellished France, the eldest daughter of the Church, whom Pope Francis greeted with this title of glory last Sunday at the Angelus and in a very moving way, given the circumstances. My own priestly vocation owes much to Saint Francis de Sales and Saint Thérèse of the Child Jesus, whose writings marked my youth, as they inspired generations of bishops, priests, and missionaries. Your invitation is for me an opportunity to thank France and to give thanks to God with you for His tradition of priestly and missionary spirituality that marked the work of the Second Vatican Ecumenical Council.

"By the ordination and mission received from the bishops," reads the preamble to the Decree *Presbyterorum Ordinis*, "priests are placed at the service of Christ the Doctor, Priest and King; they participate in his ministry which, from day to day, builds the Church here below, so that it may be the People of God, Body of Christ, Temple of the Holy Spirit."

[141] Conference for priests of the Ecclesiastical Province of Rennes, Saint Peter's Cathedral, November 20, 2015.

Friends of the Bridegroom

We are immediately introduced to the perspective of the ministry and life of priests, within the broader horizon of the ecclesiology of communion, Trinitarian and Eucharistic, of the Second Vatican Council. This prelude echoes the Dogmatic Constitution *Lumen Gentium*, which defines the sacramentality of the episcopate within the framework of the sacramentality of the Church. It is, in fact, "in Christ like a sacrament or as a sign and instrument both of a very closely knit union with God and of the unity of the whole human race."[142] Hence the meaning and importance of episcopal collegiality as a structure of communion *cum et sub Petro* in the service of the *Communio ecclesiarum*.

This great ecclesiological development in the twentieth century has made it possible to deepen the Church's evangelizing mission in the light of Her sacramental nature and thus to redefine Her relationship with the contemporary world. The Church no longer sees Herself as a "perfect society" in a position of power, capable of framing social and cultural values, as in the time of Christendom. Rather, She sees Herself as a people of believers spread among nations, a "communion" born of the Paschal Mystery of Christ. This Church is a servant of the Word and divine Life, like the Mother of the Savior. Resituated in this new context, the ministry of priests may be relativized, but, in fact, it is revalued and better integrated into the ecclesial community, notwithstanding those who believe that the Council has forgotten priests or has relegated them to the background.[143]

---

[142] *LG*, no. 1. See my interviews with Father Geoffroy de la Tousche, *Actualité et Avenir du Conseil Œcuménique Vatican II* (Dijon: L'Échelle de Jacob, 2012).

[143] Cf. Giuseppe Colombo, *Formation and Life of the Presbyter*, in Second Vatican Council, *Recezione e attualità alla luce del Giubileo*, edited by Rino Fisichella (San Paolo, 2000), pp. 551-555.

To remember the Decree on the Ministry and Life of Priests, fifty years after the conclusion of the immense event of the Council, seems to me to be a happy opportunity to recognize its prophetic value, and to extend its perspectives in the light of the pastoral and missionary conversion of the whole Church promoted by Pope Francis. The Holy Father bases this conversion and reform on the Love of Christ, Who sees and wants the Church as His holy and immaculate Bride,[144] so *semper reformanda* in the same way as Blessed Paul VI had expressed in his Encyclical *Ecclesiam Suam*.[145]

The last major intervention of Pope Francis, delivered during the celebration of the fiftieth anniversary of the institution of the Synod of Bishops, speaks of the reform of the Petrine ministry. On this occasion, the Holy Father used the image of the inverted pyramid to describe the service of the Successor of Peter in relation to the whole people of God. As *Servus servorum Dei*, the Pope is certainly recognized as the Supreme Pontiff of the Church, according to the language received, but this does not mean that he sits as a Lord at the top of the pyramid.[146] On the contrary, Francis sees himself as the first to kneel down to wash the feet of Christ's disciples, being himself first a baptized among the baptized, a bishop among the bishops, and the first among the successors of the Apostles to listen to the Holy Spirit, Who expresses Himself through the whole Church. Since his election, he has taken up

[144] Eph 5:27.

[145] Pope Francis, Apostolic Exhortation *Evangelii Gaudium*, no. 25, referring to Saint Paul VI, Encyclical Letter *Ecclesiam Suam*, August 6, 1964, nos. 10-12.

[146] "But in this Church, as in a reversed pyramid, the top is under the base. That is why those who exercise authority are called 'ministers,' because, according to the original meaning of the word, they are the smallest of all."

the theme of ministry in every way as a "service," whether Petrine, Episcopal, Presbyteral, or Diaconal.

The popular response to Pope Francis's direct and audacious words indicates the relevance of his message and the urgency for us to grasp its full scope, especially with the help of his conciliar sources, in order to listen better to what the Spirit is saying through him to the Church and the world today. His insistence on *diakonia*, which he willingly expresses in "kenotic" terms, reflects his Ignatian experience, based on a privileged identification with the Lord's Passion through the profession of the evangelical counsels. But his mystique of service comes, above all, from his understanding of the priesthood of Christ, in its dual expression, baptismal and ministerial, in the sacramental framework of the New Covenant.

How can we reread together the conciliar Decree *Presbyterorum Ordinis* fifty years after its publication? So much has happened since then in the life and ministry of priests that our gaze cannot be neutral, nor probably as enthusiastic as it was at the time. We are not unaware of the phenomenon of the secularization of society, the secularization of mentalities and mores that has decimated many Christian communities, or the recurrent polarizations that have marked either the liturgical life or the apostolic or social commitment of Christians. We are also aware that the witness of priests is still generally appreciated, but that it is more closely monitored and sometimes openly contested; and that models of participation and pastoral organization have evolved and created new conditions for the exercise of ministry in which, fortunately, laypeople play a greater part.

The list of transformations could go on, but they are sufficient to illustrate some experiences, positive or painful, that affect us closely. Each region has its own particular history and challenges; yours remind me of some of the characteristics of the Church in Quebec: loss of prestige of the priest, very aging clergy, few new members, church closures, dark sociological prospects for the future, but also a renewed hope that the Holy Father inspires by leading the whole Church into a missionary conversion that he is the first to live in full view of the world.

For the purposes of this conversation, we will first recall some aspects of the nature of the presbytery and its functions (I). We will then consider the "pastoral" conversion of priests in the horizon of the Paschal Mystery of Christ (II). Finally, we will propose, beyond the letter of the Decree but in the just hermeneutics of its potentialities, a nuptial perspective for priestly spirituality in the service of ecclesial communion.

I. The priesthood "in the sacred service of the Gospel"

Participating, for their part, in the function of the Apostles, priests receive from God the grace that makes them ministers of Christ Jesus to the nations, ensuring the sacred service of the Gospel, so that the nations may become a pleasant offering, sanctified by the Holy Spirit.[147]

A. *Nature of the priesthood*

What is a priest, and what is his mission? The Decree defines the nature of the priesthood according to the "sacred service of the Gospel"—that is, the proclamation of Jesus Christ to the nations. But it takes great care to specify, first of all, the nature of the royal

---

[147]Rom 15:16; *PO*, no. 2, §4. For some bibliographical references, cf. G. Martelet, *Deux mille ans d'Église en question*; G. Greshake, *Priester sein*; G. Colombo, *Teologia sacramentaria* (Milan: Glossa, 1997), pp. 415-522; Hervé Legrand, "Presbytre/Prêtre," in Jean-Yves Lacoste, ed., *Dictionnaire critique de théologie* (Paris: Quadrige PUF, 2007), pp. 1117-1118.

priesthood, which is of all the baptized, because of their belonging to the Body of Christ:

> The Lord Jesus, "whom the Father has sanctified and sent into the world" (Jn 10:36), makes all his Mystical Body participate in the anointing of the Spirit that he has received (cf. Mt 3:16; Lk 4:18; Acts 4:27; 10:38).... There is therefore no member who does not have his part in the mission of the whole Body; there is no one who should not sanctify Jesus in his heart and give witness to Jesus through the spirit of prophecy.[148]

This starting point of the Decree is essential because it applies to priests the ecclesiological turn of the Second Vatican Council, which speaks first of the people of God, then of the hierarchical constitution of the Church, by defining more clearly the purpose of the ministerial priesthood according to the royal priesthood: "Indeed, the apostolic proclamation of the Gospel convokes and gathers the People of God so that all the members of this people, being sanctified by the Holy Spirit, 'offer themselves as a living sacrifice, holy, acceptable to God' (Rom 12:1)."[149] This priestly character of all the people of God is brought to fulfillment through the ministry of priests through whom the spiritual sacrifice of Christians is consummated, in union with the sacrifice of Christ, "offered in the name of the whole Church in the Eucharist by the hands of priests."[150]

The Decree obviously reminds us that the hierarchical priesthood is based on the Sacrament of Holy Orders, "which, by the anointing of the Holy Spirit, marks them with a special character

[148]PO, no. 2, §1.
[149]PO, no. 2, §4.
[150]Ibid.

and configures them to Christ the Priest to enable them to act in the name of Christ the Head in person."[151] It is further defined as the "sacred power to offer the Sacrifice and to forgive sins" and its own function, "as it is united to the episcopal order, participates in the authority by which Christ himself builds, sanctifies and governs his Body."[152] In short, the hierarchical priesthood is a specific sacramental mediation that is related to the common priesthood of the baptized in order to accomplish a mystery of communion: the Church of God, where Christ the Head offers Himself to the Father with His Body of the baptized, and where the Father responds with the outpouring of the Holy Spirit upon the world, all lived in fullness in the Eucharist through the ministry of priests united to their bishop.

This complementarity of the royal and ministerial priesthoods reminds me of the experience I had in the Archdiocese of Quebec City, thanks to the 2008 International Eucharistic Congress. The organization of this event mobilized all the living forces of the diocese in a way that made us aware that the mission of a diocese is realized in the communion of the communities of a territory around the Eucharist. Whether these communities are parish, religious, or apostolic, the fundamental principle is the living witness of Baptism in whose service everything is directed, beginning with the ministry of the bishop and his presbytery. A logo of overlapping concentric circles, articulated on the model of the Holy Trinity, then became the symbol of our witness of communion as a way of living the evangelizing mission of the local Church or, if you will, its sacramentality in relation to the world.

This global vision of mission as a "communion of communities" in which everyone finds his place had a significant effect on the

---

[151] *PO*, no. 2, §3.
[152] Ibid.

motivation of priests, the witness of men and women religious, and the apostolate of the movements. Rivalries were reduced, to the benefit of the recognition of charisms and their more harmonious integration, with the help of pastors capable of this discernment. The climate became more joyful and fraternal, thus helping priests to show the human qualities that the Decree recommends, "kindness, sincerity, moral strength, perseverance, passion for justice, delicacy."[153]

B. Priests, ministers of the Word of God and the sacraments

Chapter II of *Presbyterorum Ordinis* details the functions of priests, beginning with their activity as ministers of the Word of God. "The people of God are gathered first of all by the Word of the living God, which is to be expected especially from priests (Cf. 1 Pet. 1:23; Acts 6:7; 12:34)."[154] Whether this Word be proclaimed by priests to unbelievers or Christian communities, in any case, "it is a question for them to teach, not their own wisdom, but the word of God, and to invite all men with insistence to conversion and holiness."[155] The Decree recognizes that this priestly preaching, in the present state of the world, "is often very difficult"; if it is to reach the minds of the listeners, it must not be content with exposing the word of God in a general and abstract way, but "applying the permanent truth of the Gospel to the concrete circumstances of life."[156] Pope Francis gives us a good example of this at daily Mass in Santa Marta. Our ministry of the Word is often exercised in front of nonpracticing Catholics or unbelievers who occasionally come to church for funerals or weddings. Let us then resist the temptation to lower the

[153] PO, no. 3, §1.
[154] PO, no. 4, §1.
[155] Ibid.
[156] Ibid.

level of preaching and dare to announce the kerygma that has in itself a grace to touch and convert hearts.

Relying on the Constitution *Sacrosanctum Concilium*, on the liturgy, the Council Fathers then drew particular attention to the celebration of the Word of God in the liturgy, "where the proclamation of the Lord's death and resurrection, the response of the people who listen to it, the very oblation of Christ sealing in his blood the New Covenant, and the communion of Christians to this oblation through prayer and the reception of the sacrament are inseparably united."[157] The restoration of the homily, including its mystagogical character, certainly represents one of the major advances of the Second Vatican Council, supported by a renewed sense of the permanent relevance of the Word of God, in connection with the conviction that priests act "in sacred celebrations as ministers of the One who, through his Spirit, constantly exercises his priestly function for us, in the liturgy."[158]

This permanence of the exercise of Christ's priestly function in the liturgy gives rise in the Decree to one of the most beautiful developments in conciliar thought on the Eucharist. It deserves our attention: "For the Holy Eucharist contains all the spiritual treasure of the Church, that is, Christ himself, our Passover, the living bread, him whose flesh, vivified by the Holy and life-giving Spirit, gives life to men, inviting them and leading them to offer, in union with him, their own life, their work, all creation."[159] This is why, the text continues, "The Eucharist is indeed the source and summit of all evangelization"; catechumens are gradually led there, and Christians, baptized and confirmed, find there "their full insertion in the Body of Christ."[160]

---

[157] *PO*, no. 4, §2.
[158] *PO*, no. 5, §1.
[159] *PO*, no. 5, §2.
[160] Ibid.

It follows that "it is the Eucharistic assembly which is the center of the Christian community presided over by the priest,"[161] an affirmation that in no way diminishes the importance of the celebration around the bishop, but firmly roots ecclesiology in the basic Eucharistic community presided over by the priest. This ecclesiological option has a great ecumenical significance, especially in relation to the Orthodox who introduced their Eucharistic ecclesiology to the Council.[162] "Priests, therefore, teach Christians to offer the divine victim to God the Father in the sacrifice of the Mass, and to make with him the offering of their lives";[163] for this purpose, they help them to cultivate the necessary dispositions: the spirit of penance and prayer as well as the praise and thanksgiving whose Eucharistic dimension the priests themselves extend through the faithful recitation of the Divine Office.

This year, revisiting the figure of the holy Curé d'Ars on the occasion of the two hundredth anniversary of his priestly ordination, I was struck by a relatively forgotten aspect of his holiness: the fact that he converted his parish. God knows that he prayed, fasted, and suffered for this intention! Ars did not have a good reputation. This neglected periphery of the diocese of Lyon initially resisted its demands and would have gladly pushed it elsewhere, but after ten years of fierce spiritual struggle, he could count on a transformed parish, which not only loved its priest but was ready to mobilize to prevent him from leaving. This is the holy covenant of a holy

---

[161] PO, no. 5, §3.

[162] Cf. Jean Zizioulas, Alexandre Schmemann, and especially Nicolas Afanassief, quoted in the Acta Sinodalia of the Council. See Walter Kasper, Ecclesiology of the Eucharist: From Vatican II to Sacramentum Caritatis, Proceedings of the International Symposium of Theology, International Eucharistic Congress of Quebec, June 11-13, 2008, pp. 194ff.

[163] PO, no. 5, §3.

priest with his people: a common witness of the pastor giving his life for his sheep, through his vigils, his mercy, his penances, his tender devotion to the Virgin Mary, and a community that allows itself to be touched by his example and his word, that prays, confesses, and converts itself until the change in morals occurs. The priesthood of the Curé d'Ars is glorious because he has invested himself totally in the holiness of his flock.

C. *Priests, leaders of God's people*

Thirdly, the Decree speaks of priests as pastors, that is, as leaders of the people of God. They exercise, at their level of authority, the function of Christ the Head and Shepherd: "In the name of the bishop, they unite the family of God, the community of brothers who live a dynamism of unity, and they lead it through Christ in the Spirit to God the Father."[164] Let us note here again the Trinitarian inspiration that dwells in these texts, which consequently leads to particular accents for the pastoral conduct of priests. They must show extreme humanity (*eximia humanitate*), following the example of the Lord, and be gentle and humble of heart, friend of the poor and merciful to all sinners.

In this spirit, priests have at heart to be for all, the Decree emphasizes, but they will pay special attention to the poor and the little ones: "The Lord has shown, indeed, that he himself has a part bound with them, and their evangelization is given as a sign of the messianic work."[165] This conciliar orientation given to all priests is taken up and brought to the forefront, as we know, by the actions and words of Pope Francis. The pastoral conversion of the priests he wishes for certainly requires individual generosity towards the poor, but it is, above all, aimed at fostering a true community spirit

[164] *PO*, no. 6, §1.
[165] *PO*, no. 6, §3.

of charity and solidarity. This applies first and foremost to the unity of the presbytery around the bishop. What is more important in the present circumstances than the communion and fraternity of priests among themselves and around the bishop, beyond the differences of generations and spiritual, liturgical, and pastoral sensibilities?

Consequently, the function of guide or pastor must not be exercised in isolation or in an autocratic way but in communion with all, in particular by virtue of the "very unity of consecration and mission [that] requires their hierarchical communion with the Order of Bishops."[166] This unity "leads the bishops to consider priests as brothers and friends, and to concern themselves, as much as they can, with their material good first and foremost, but especially with their spiritual good."[167] Hence their "grave responsibility for the holiness of their priests," which implies an active commitment to the "ongoing spiritual formation of their presbyterium,"[168] as well as to its participation in the government of the diocese through appropriate structures and councils. Conversely, communion between priests and the bishop is expressed "in charity and obedience"; it is extended in the "sacramental fraternity" between the members of the same presbytery, which is refined by charity, cooperation, hospitality, and fraternal correction.

With regard to the laity, priests do not forget that they are "brothers among their brothers" in the one "Body of Christ whose construction has been entrusted to all."[169] "Testing the spirits to know if they are of God (1 Jn 4:1), they will know how to discover and discern in faith the charisms of the laity in all their forms, from the most modest to the most elevated; they will recognize them

[166] *PO*, no. 7, §1.
[167] Ibid.
[168] Ibid.
[169] *PO*, no. 9, §1.

with joy and develop them with ardour."[170] These are, therefore, some of the doctrinal aspects of the Decree that thus lay the foundations for a "spirituality of communion" which priests cannot do without, if they want to know the joy of evangelizing and face more serenely the challenges of the individualistic and narcissistic culture of our time.

II. For a "pastoral" spirituality in a "kenotic" mode
A. A particular call to holiness

Chapter III of the Decree *Presbyterorum Ordinis* on the spirituality of priests is solemnly introduced to indicate that the message addressed here to priests explicitly commits the aims of the conciliar assembly:

> To achieve its pastoral goal of inner renewal of the Church, of spreading the Gospel throughout the world and of dialogue with the world today, (this holy Council) urges all priests to remember that with the help of the adapted means that the Church offers them, they must strive to live more and more a holiness that will make them ever more suitable instruments in the service of the whole people of God.[171]

This call to holiness concerns priests in a particular capacity, because of their consecration by the Sacrament of Orders: "As soon as he holds in his own way the place of Christ in person, every priest is, therefore, endowed with a particular grace, which allows him to tend more easily… towards the perfection of the One he represents."[172] At this point, the Council formulates one of its essential orientations for the unity of the spiritual life of priests: "It is

[170] PO, no. 9, §2.
[171] PO, no. 12, §4.
[172] Ibid.

99

the faithful, tireless exercise of their functions in the Spirit of Christ which is, for priests, the authentic means to achieve holiness."[173]

Much has been written about this formula. It was seen as an undoubted progress in priestly spirituality compared with previous conceptions inspired either by religious or monastic life or by the practice of spiritual exercises. In principle and in fact, the spiritual life of priests does not have to develop alongside and in spite of their ministry, but in it, starting from the principle of unity, which is Christ Himself exercising His pastoral charity in them and through them.

Number 14 of the Decree explicitly poses the problem of the unity of the spiritual life of priests, recognizing that they are torn between multiple obligations and that they cannot succeed only through rational management of their agenda or by "the sole practice of pious exercises," which are certainly important. The key always remains union with Christ in the exercise of ministry: "Leading the very life of the Good Shepherd in this way, they will find in the exercise of pastoral charity the bond of priestly perfection that will bring their life and action back to unity."[174] It is then quickly repeated that "this pastoral charity derives above all from the Eucharistic Sacrifice; this is therefore the center and root of the whole life of the priest, whose priestly spirit strives to interiorize what is done on the altar of sacrifice."[175]

B. Pastoral charity in kenotic mode

Two virtues are highlighted to illustrate what it means to exercise pastoral charity in a kenotic mode: humility and obedience. "The true minister of Christ is [therefore] a man conscious of his

---

[173] PO, no. 13, §1.
[174] PO, no. 14, §2.
[175] Ibid.

weakness, working in humility, discerning what pleases the Lord; chained, so to speak, by the Spirit, he lets himself be led in everything by the will of the One who wants all men to be saved."[176] Priests practice humility and obedience by appropriating "the sentiments of Jesus Christ,"[177] who "emptied himself, taking on the form of a servant ... becoming obedient even to death."[178]

Returning to the image of the inverted pyramid used by Francis to describe his own Petrine spirituality, I notice that it is rooted in the scene of the washing of feet, with explicitly Eucharistic connotations. In my opinion, this confirms a traditional, sacrificial aspect of priestly spirituality, in a symbolic language that is in line with the theology of the Church Fathers.[179]

The Good Shepherd gives his life for his sheep.[180] This is the charter *par excellence* of priestly spirituality, which is rooted

[176] *PO*, no. 15, §1.

[177] Phil 2:7-8.

[178] Phil 2:9; *PO*, no. 15, §4.

[179] See Origen, Homily on the Judges: "Come, please, Lord Jesus, Son of God, 'strip yourself of the clothes' that you have put on for me, 'pour water into a basin and wash the feet' of your servants. Remove the filth of your sons and daughters. 'Wash the feet' of our soul, so that in your imitation and following you, 'we will get rid of' our old 'clothes.' ... So now I too want to 'wash the feet' of my brothers, 'wash the feet' of my classmates.... Yes, to the best of my ability, I desire to 'wash the feet' of my brothers, and to fulfill the command of the Lord.... Thus, all together in Christ, purified by his word, we will not be rejected from the Bridegroom's wedding feast in the sight of unclean clothing, but in white clothing, washed feet and 'pure of heart,' we will take our place at the feast of the Bridegroom, our Lord Jesus Christ in person, 'to whom belong the glory and power for ever and ever. Amen.'" Trans. P. Messié, L. Neyrand, and M. Borret, *Sources Chrétiennes*, no. 389 (Paris: éd. du Cerf, 1993).

[180] Cf. Jn 10:10.

in the heart of Trinitarian Life: "This is why the Father loves me, because I give my life.... I have the power to give it and the power to take it back; this is the command I have received from my Father."[181] For the Father has given Him to have Life in Himself and to give it abundantly in the economy of salvation, in a kenotic, Eucharistic form, for the life of the world. Revelation describes this paradox with powerful images of abyss and glory, purification and victory, thanks to the privileged figure of the sacrificed and victorious Lamb: "The Lamb who stands in the midst of the throne will be their shepherd and will lead them to the springs of the waters of life,"[182] thus indicating that He continues to guide His people, from His superhuman glorious condition, and at the same time by the poor and humble signs of His sacramental manifestation.

As the sacrificed and victorious Lamb, the Good Shepherd continues to give Himself through the priests who administer these sacramental signs, glorifying God His Father with Him and procuring salvation for humanity. They incarnate His pastoral charity, in a spirit of service, without dominating the faithful, letting themselves be led by the One Who commands their word, their actions, and their sacrifices from His last place on the Cross and in the Eucharist, "the spiritual treasure of the Church."[183]

C. From the Eucharist, the eschatological center of gravity

The Word of the risen Christ, therefore, continues to dwell in human history through the ministry of the priests, who are prophets, not by virtue of a power they have over it, but conversely, by virtue of the power that the Word has over them, by virtue of their

---

[181] Jn 10:17-18.
[182] Rev 7:17.
[183] PO, no. 5, §2.

sacramental ordination *ad sacerdotium* — that is, for the celebration of the Holy Sacrifice of the Paschal Lamb. To go to the bottom of the symbol of the inverted pyramid of which Pope Francis speaks, we priests and bishops must understand that our lives, like those of Mary and the Twelve Apostles, is radically "under the Word," attracted and possessed by it, requisitioned to be its instruments, in order to attract by it all humanity into the eschatological center of gravity of the Holy Eucharist.

When we celebrate the Holy Eucharist and pronounce the words of consecration in their own context, we experience the fullness of our priesthood as ministers of Christ the Lord. The Word of Christ that we pronounce, this divine Word that first "created the worlds,"[184] and "now makes all things new,"[185] then emerges at the heart of our humble daily lives as a transcendent, eschatological reality, although lacking in brilliance. This Word is not "repeated" by us as if it were changeable at will; it is "pronounced" as a divine Word given "once and for all." In pronouncing it, we do not multiply it and we do not fragment it; rather, we are challenged and supported by its suprahistorical relevance for its service. Through and for this service in the power of the Holy Spirit, we accomplish the ritual gestures and pronounce all the words that surround this "Paschal Mystery," conscious to varying degrees that our ministry and our life then express, poorly but truly, the very Heart of Christ: the humble and victorious Trinitarian Love, all the more glorious and more deeply hidden in its lowering.

Indeed, Christ's gift to the Father through obedience of love until death is the supreme manifestation of His glory. This gift takes a *kenotic* form not only "for a time," because of humanity's sinful condition, as if the event of His Resurrection then made "kenosis"

---

[184] Heb 1:2.
[185] Rev 21:5.

a reality of the past and therefore outdated. In fact, the opposite is true. The Resurrection of Christ confirms everything; it does not cancel anything of His sacrifice and therefore of His kenosis, but rather, it glorifies them as the *holy mystery* of Trinitarian Love in its temporal form of immolation, which is, moreover, the transposition of His eternal and absolute self-giving into Himself. The Resurrection of Christ by the power of the Holy Spirit therefore places the ultimate Trinitarian seal of divine Life on His flesh, glorifying it, making it "pneumatic," Eucharistic, and thus life-giving for sinful humanity.[186] This Trinitarian Life is an absolute gift, a reciprocal gift, and a threefold fruitful one, a gift that Revelation celebrates triumphantly with the help of the symbol of the Wedding of the Lamb. This is why all the activity of priests, of the bishop, of diocesan communities, of the whole Church is aspired, assumed, polarized, magnetized by this source and this summit of sacramental communion that marries Heaven and earth.[187]

The Second Vatican Council did not, therefore, sacrifice anything of the priest's identity; on the contrary, it promoted it as never before, restoring the ministry of the Word against the background of a deeper theology of Revelation in the light of the Paschal Mystery of Christ.[188] Moreover, by framing it through the development of the sacramentality of the episcopate in an ecclesiology of communion, potentially Eucharistic, the Council

[186] See M. Ouellet, "L'Esprit dans la vie trinitaire," in the *Revue Catholique Internationale Communio*, no. 23, 1-2 (January-April 1998), pp. 39-53.

[187] See the Exultet of the Easter Vigil.

[188] See Second Vatican Council, Dogmatic Constitution on Divine Revelation *Dei Verbum*, no. 2: "The profound truth about God as well as about the salvation of man is through this revelation that it shines before our eyes in Christ, who is both the mediator and the fullness of the whole revelation."

has extraordinarily enriched the identity of the priest and the importance of his pastoral ministry at the heart of the Christian community. He made the priest a "man of communion," at the service of the fraternal and missionary communion of the Church, drawing daily with full hands from the Eucharistic source of Trinitarian communion. In this light, priests have no reason to become jaded and grumpy officials; they have every reason to rejoice that the ministry of the Spirit is so powerfully at work in their humble obedience.

Unfortunately, the Decree was not immediately taken into account, placing it in this overall vision, to the point that some wrote that the priests had been forgotten, then caught up at the last minute, thanks to these few paragraphs. It was thus superficially believed that, in order to avoid a crisis that we sensed, it was necessary to reaffirm some known truths and disciplines, such as the sacrificial nature of the Eucharist, the importance of the daily Mass for the priest, the confirmation of the law of celibacy, obedience, and humility as fundamental virtues that allow the bishops to keep priests under control. This superficial interpretation does not do justice to the Council, which has profoundly rethought the ministry and life of priests from the Paschal Mystery of Christ and in the perspective of Trinitarian and ecclesial communion.

This redesign is confirmed by the relational openness it commands in all directions, starting with the prayer life of priests, their fraternal and institutional relationships, and their pastoral creativity, which generates not only holy souls but also living and missionary Christian communities. If it is true that the priest is ordained to the service of the Incarnate Word in His glorious kenosis, to the service of Love, which goes to the end of His Trinitarian bestowal, is he not then mandated and equipped to render the greatest and most beautiful possible service to humanity? How, then, can his activity and his whole life not be possessed by this eternal

Life offered to his faith, entrusted to his care, and begging for his commitment? How can he lose sight of the wonderful dignity of his fatherly, filial, and fraternal mediation, for the benefit of the communities he serves and who live by his testimony?

III. So that the world may believe in Love

A. *The priest, sacrament of Christ, Head and Spouse*

This is all very well and good, you may say, but at this point in the local churches, struggling with the difficulties of families and the education of young people, with the scarcity of vocations, the anthropological crisis, the parishes without priests, one would be tempted either to give up or to tinker with quick solutions to meet needs, sometimes at the risk of missing the real challenges. How can we revive our hope as pastors in the face of an indifferent or hostile world that no longer seems to vibrate when the Christian mystery is announced? Without ignoring these haunting challenges, I believe that hope is and will always be reborn from the appropriation of the mystery of love that is the priesthood. "The priesthood is the Love of the Heart of Jesus," the Curé d'Ars gladly repeated. Its formula applies as much to the common priesthood as to the ministerial priesthood and precisely calls for the encounter of two loves.

In this respect, a fruitful spiritual perspective, but not very present in the Decree, emerges in my opinion from the "many conveniences" that the Decree recalls between the priesthood and the celibacy of priests:

In this way they profess themselves before men as willing to be dedicated to the office committed to them—namely, to commit themselves faithfully to one man and to show themselves as a chaste virgin for Christ and thus to evoke the mysterious marriage established by Christ, and fully to

be manifested in the future, in which the Church has Christ
as her only Spouse.[189]

This nuptial theme is not very developed by the Council, but it
will be largely developed during the pontificate of Saint John Paul
II, in particular to better justify, from the sacramental point of view,
that women are not called to exercise the ordained ministry. But
above all, it is fruitful in order to confer an emotional and symbolic
flavor to conjugal, priestly, and even religious spirituality. This is
why I am speaking about it here, while being aware that I am going
beyond the letter of the Decree in the direction of hermeneutics
that the sovereign pontiffs, especially John Paul II, have developed
on this point in relation to priestly spirituality.

We know the importance of the bridal symbolism in the Bible,
which reveals the mystery of the Covenant between God and His
people. This symbolism crosses the whole of Sacred Scripture, from
Genesis to Revelation, with the Paschal Mystery of Christ as its
center of gravity and the Song of Songs as the hermeneutical key.
The writings of Saint Paul and Saint John adopt it significantly to
express the relationship between Christ and the Church, which
will be taken up and fed into a whole literature of the patristic,
Greek, Syriac, and even Latin traditions.[190] It contains the image
of the Bridegroom applied first to God, then to Christ, and even
to the bishop as the representative of Christ the Bridegroom in
His relationship with the Church. The Christian East will keep
this theological tradition alive, while in the West it will survive
mainly thanks to the mystical tradition; more recently, several
artisans of biblical and patristic renewal will give it pride of place,

[189] PO, no. 16, §2; LG, no. 21; *Perfectae Caritatis*, no. 12; cf. also Saint
John Chrysostom, *De sacerdotio*, 3, 6, where the priest is described
as the one "whose task is to beautify the bride of Christ."
[190] Think of Origen, Ephrem, Jacob of Sarug, and Augustine.

thus preparing for the magisterial deepening.[191] John Paul II systematically integrates it into his catechesis on human love, marriage, and the family, consecrated life, priestly and even episcopal ministry.[192]

Commenting on the priest's spirituality in the light of the figure of the Good Shepherd, John Paul II deepens pastoral charity in explicitly nuptial terms. He writes: "The gift that Christ makes of himself to his Church, the fruit of his love, takes on the original meaning of the husband's own gift to his wife, as the sacred texts suggest more than once. Jesus is the true bridegroom, who offers the wine of salvation to the Church (cf. Jn 2:11). He who is 'the Head of the Church,... the Savior of the Body' (Eph 5:23), 'loved the Church and gave himself up for her" (Eph 5:26-27).[193] The Holy Father then goes on with the same image applied to the priest, configured to Christ the Bridegroom, who is therefore "in the Church but also in front of the Church," called in his spiritual life to relive the love of Christ the Bridegroom towards the Church, the Bride:

> His life must therefore be illuminated and guided by this spousal character which requires him to be a witness of Christ's spousal love, so that he will be able to love people with a new, great and pure heart, with an authentic detachment from himself, in a total, continuous and faithful self giving. And he will experience it as divine "jealousy" (cf. 2 Cor 11:2), with a tenderness that even adorns itself with the nuances of maternal affection, capable of bearing the

---

[191] In particular, the work of Henri de Lubac, Hugo Rahner, Hans Urs von Balthasar, Louis Bouyer, M. J. Le Guillou, etc.

[192] Saint John Paul II, *Familiaris Consortio*, *Mulieris Dignitatem*, *Pastores Dabo Vobis*, *Pastores Gregis*.

[193] *PDV*, no. 22.

"pains of childbirth" until "Christ is formed" in the faithful (cf. Gal 4:19).[194]

The same idea is forcefully taken up by the Holy Father as the ultimate motivation to confirm the Church's willingness to maintain the law of ecclesiastical celibacy:

> The Church, as Spouse of Jesus Christ, wants to be loved by the priest in the total and exclusive way in which Jesus Christ Head and Spouse loved her. Priestly celibacy, then, is a gift of self in and with Christ to his Church, and it expresses the service rendered by the priest to the Church in and with the Lord.[195]

B. The Virgin Mary and the fullness of the priesthood

These magnificent texts are well known and speak for themselves. They deserve to be taken up and internalized, especially in the current context, where the meaning of nuptiality is confused, if not perverted, by theories and practices that are contrary to Christian doctrine. Before I conclude, I would like to add to this nuptial perspective a final Marian consideration aimed at rooting even more deeply the spirit of service that priests, together with their bishop, laypeople, and people of consecrated life, are called to interiorize for a profound missionary conversion.

I recalled at the very beginning with *Presbyterorum Ordinis* that priests are ordained for the service of the royal priesthood of the baptized, which consists essentially in the practice of the theological virtues and sacraments to serve, in their own way and at their own level, the glorification of God and the salvation of humanity. I now believe it is possible to attempt to unify the two "essentially

---

[194] PDV, no. 22.
[195] PDV, no. 29.

different" modes of participation in the one priesthood of Christ on the basis of the Trinitarian fecundity, which is expressed and participated in, in a variety of ways in the complementarity of the common priesthood and the hierarchical priesthood.

Let us begin with the most fundamental participation, that of the Virgin Mary, who receives and gives to the world the Word, this Word that she gives birth to and accompanies throughout all the phases of the Incarnation, until the supreme expression of the Paschal Mystery. Totally subordinate to the only Mediator, Mary is totally associated with Him in love, and remains forever fruitful in Him as Mother of God and Spouse of the sacrificed Lamb. Her divine motherhood and her spiritual motherhood at the Cross constitute the fullness of the common priesthood as a nuptial participation in the priesthood of Christ. Her unreserved and unconditional welcome, as well as her unfailing service of Trinitarian fruitfulness in the power of the Holy Spirit, constitute the origin and permanent foundation of the Church's priesthood as Spouse of the living God. The faithful people instinctively perceive this fullness of the mediation of Mary, Mother of the Church, and express it in a thousand ways in popular devotions. "O Jesus, living in Mary, come and live in your servants."[196]

Let us now take one more step. Within and in the service of this Trinitarian fecundity, which gives itself a nuptial figure in the relationship between Christ and the Church, there is necessarily the function of representing Christ the Bridegroom in front of the Bride, the Church. Indeed, the mission of Christ the Bridegroom consists not only in sharing His life as Son but also in communicating the life of the Spirit and that of the Father, Who sends Him. Hence the origin of the "apostolic," "ministerial," or "hierarchical" priesthood, which sacramentally incarnates the love of

---

[196] Jean-Jacques Olier's prayer, dear to the Sulpician tradition.

Christ the Bridegroom as it represents the Father in the economy of salvation. The hierarchical priesthood is the sacramental sign of the "original" nuptial love of the Father, which is joined to the "original" nuptial love of Christ, both of them professing with one breath the fullness of Life of the Spirit, which contains the infinite fruitfulness of the three divine Persons. In the economy of salvation, the Father's Originating Love generates and makes God's children grow in Christ; it associates in Him the filial love of the baptized as His Body and Spouse, to inspire and con-spire together the Spirit of Trinitarian communion in the heart of the world. The whole mystery of the priesthood as a meeting of two loves is ultimately focused on the communication of the divine Spirit to the world, to convert it, sanctify it, and finally glorify it in the unity of Trinitarian love. "As you, Father, are in me and I in you, may they also be in us, that the world may believe that you have sent me ... and that you have loved them as you have loved me."[197]

As an expression of authentic participation in intra-Trinitarian communion, the two sacramental forms of Christ's one priesthood correspond and strengthen each other in a way that allows the glory of God in the Life of the Spirit to be reflected in the Christian community, spread in hearts and in ecclesial relationships. Hence its fruitfulness in the free and generous charity of Christians, in the "communion of communities," in the mutual love and therefore the joy of the faith lived, in the graces and charisms spread for the mission, to which are added the free miracles, the missionary adventures, the testimonies of martyrs — in a word, the Church, sacrament of the Trinitarian communion in the heart of the world — for its hope and salvation.

[197] Jn 17:21, 23.

Friends of the Bridegroom

The priests of the New Covenant, sons of Mary, Mediatrix of all graces, are witnesses, heralds, and leading craftsmen of these divine wonders. They are the first to be coordinated in the pastoral and missionary conversion of the Church, in communion with lay people and consecrated persons, and especially with their bishop, *cum et sub Petro*. Nothing can better serve the mission of the local Church than the bonds of fruitful communion among all who make the world discover the true face of God and the eternal life of the Kingdom already begun on earth.

Conclusion

The Council Decree *Presbyterorum Ordinis*, which we have just reviewed and commented on in the context of conciliar ecclesiology, manifests its prophetic character through the fundamental role it recognizes for priests, cooperators of the Episcopal Order, in the service of the sacramentality of the Church, mystery of communion. As representatives of Christ the Head, the presbyters exercise their pastoral functions from the Eucharistic mystery, which totally requisitions their persons, their words, and their lives in the service of the nuptial love of Christ and the Church. Hence the need for baptismal and ministerial holiness, which requires from them an intense spirituality, a true "mystique of relationships," marked by dialogue and filial, fraternal, and paternal love, at the service of the Church, Which evangelizes through the attraction of Her missionary communion.

The prophetic character of this conciliar document is certainly evident in the restoration of the ministry of the Word, especially in a liturgical context, but it emanates, above all, from the kenotic accent of the spirituality of priests, supported by the Easter relevance of Christ's gift "once and for all" in the Eucharist. In this light, the Decree explicitly calls priests to a privileged commitment to the poor, the sick, and the marginalized, thus prolonging the Eucharistic love of the Lord through His *diakonia* with the poor, a fundamental trait that returns in force under the providential impulse of the Holy Father in the dramatic hours in which we are living.

The horizon of nuptial theology that we mentioned in conclusion, following in the footsteps of Saint John Paul II, seems to me to be faithful to the spirit of the Decree, even if it goes beyond the limits of his letter. This encompassing horizon is barely sketched out, but it seems fruitful to me to encourage priests to be "fathers," to generate vocations, to promote a "revolution of tenderness," in the manner of Pope Francis. What more beautiful, indeed, and joyful vocation than to serve Christ the Bridegroom in His outpouring of love for the Church, so that She may become ever more Bride and fruitful Mother, missionary like the Virgin of the Annunciation, the Visitation, and Pentecost, bringing to the world the joy of the Gospel of salvation. May God bless you and renew you in this joy!

* * *

Jesus was in the temple every day to teach … and all the people, hanging on his words, listened to him.[198]

Dear friends, bishops, priests, deacons, laity, and consecrated persons,

At the end of these days of retreat and reflection in a priestly encounter, which extends the dimensions of the Ecclesiastical Province, and within a national context disrupted by terrorist madness, our first instinct is to stick together around the altar, in the fraternal communion and national solidarity that inspire our faith and pastoral charity. We are bruised by these painful events; we wish to be silent and pray. Lord have mercy! *Kyrie eleison!* Listen

---

[198]Lk 19:47-48. Homily at a retreat for priests of the province of Rennes, November 20, 2015.

to Jesus and pray. Jesus tells us about the Father and His house of prayer. The Father also speaks to us through Jesus. Let us listen to Him! Our bruised hearts and humiliated minds will be comforted and encouraged to go back on the road.

In this series preceding the solemnity of Christ the King, the Word of God presents us with two contrasting scenes concerning the true worship of God. The first book of the Martyrs of Israel speaks of the new dedication of the Temple, in a festive atmosphere, after the victory over the enemies who had desecrated the altar and the temple through their idolatrous worship. "And the altar was dedicated to the singing of hymns, and to the sound of the zitars, harps, and cymbals, . . . offering burnt offerings, and sacrifices of communion and thanksgiving, with joy."[199] We understand their legitimate joy because "the humiliation inflicted by the pagans was erased."[200]

In Luke's Gospel, on the contrary, we see the scene where Jesus expels the sellers from the Temple and declares: "My house will be a house of prayer, but you have made it a den of bandits."[201] These are hard words that testify to Jesus' passion for His Father's house and for the true worship He expects from man: a cult not only of the lips but of the whole being, heart, soul, and body.

In the parallel passages, Jesus adds the word concerning the temple of His own body: "Destroy this temple and in three days I will raise it up."[202] This language appears cryptic to His disciples, but it becomes luminous for the Church after His Resurrection from the dead. This prophetic word makes us understand that the place of true worship of the living God is the temple of His glorified body, to which we are united by Baptism, which makes

[199] 1 Macc 4:56.
[200] 1 Macc 4:58.
[201] Lk 19:46.
[202] Jn 2:19.

us members of His Body. In this temple of His Body, which is the Church, our prayer unites with His to the point of becoming one with His sacrificial offering, by virtue of the gifts of the common priesthood and the ministerial priesthood. The celebration of the Holy Eucharist is the exercise *par excellence* of this double and unique priesthood, for it raises to God the prayer of Jesus Christ in the name of all humanity, and in return it obtains the abundance of grace that the Father brings down upon the Church and the world by the power of His Spirit.

Aware of the salvific value of this mystery, we ask today for the grace of a renewed faith in this incomparable and indivisible wonder of the Eucharist and the priesthood. On this solemn occasion, which reminds us in some way of the Chrism Mass, we ask for the grace of a new dedication of the temples of our bodies and of all our faculties in the service of the Body of Christ, which is the Church. The bread of sacrifice that we take in our hands to consecrate, consume, and distribute to the faithful, this sacramental Body of the Lord, nourishes the Body and Soul of His Spouse, the Church. We are the friends of the Bridegroom: do we not wish to dedicate ourselves even more deeply to His Bride, Whom He also loves through us with an unfailing love? May this renewal of our promises as friends of the Bridegroom include the whole Church, the community entrusted to us, the Presbyterium and the dioceses to which we belong, and the whole nation within the catholicity of the Church.

France has known other dark times in its history, and it has been able to respond and draw on its deepest spiritual resources to bounce back, rebuild itself, and relaunch the missionary adventure. What would spiritual France be like today without Ars, Lourdes, and Lisieux? From where can we rebound and rebuild ourselves if not from the ministry of mercy made famous by the Holy Father, from the tenderness of the Mother of Mercy at the Massabielle fountain, or from the offering of holocaust to the merciful love of the Father of Thérèse of the Child Jesus and the Holy Face, the little bride of Christ who delights in the one Name of Jesus.

At the time of the Jubilee of Mercy proclaimed by Pope Francis, let us draw on these precious resources, and at the same time revive fraternal charity and social solidarity. A sacred union for national security, of course, but also the reception of refugees, interreligious dialogue, and, despite the increased tensions of this nonconventional wartime, a coexistence that respects differences of all kinds. The field is wide open for the pastoral conversion of our priestly, parish, religious, apostolic, and diocesan communities.

May the love of the Lord be our prophetic witness, a tender and merciful love, but also engaged in the struggles for justice and peace, a courageous love rooted in history and witnessing the pride of our spiritual and cultural roots, as the historical theme park Puy-du-Fou invites us to do in this territory.

Dear bishops of the Ecclesiastical Province of Rennes, the sign of unity that we have of the joy of living together is a sign of the times, a prophetic message to bring to a society in disarray and confusion, longing deeply for the consolation of hope. Your initiative will bear fruit in each of your dioceses, because your bonds of deep communion with the Holy Father will strengthen the sacramental fraternity of priests, and it will be a source of vocations to the priestly ministry that we cherish.

Dear priests of the Most High God, who love with all your heart the One who has become the lowliest, in the last place of the glorious Cross, may your pastoral charity follow the same path of Love that becomes daily bread and abundant drink for your brothers and sisters in faith. Let us pray and do penance for the conversion of our parishes; let us take our young people to Lourdes or on pilgrimage to Notre-Dame de Chartres or to the diocesan sanctuary; let us love the poor and the sick as the privileged of the

Lord; and let our desire for holiness be intense but detached from ourselves and turned towards our people.

Dear members of the faithful people, let us thank God for the charisms He grants to our communities, but let us rejoice above all in being children of God through Baptism. This grace is the most excellent grace there is; it establishes and justifies a hierarchical priesthood at its service, for the edification of the Body of Christ. Let us thank God together for being loved by Him personally, and also for serving Him by loving one another, nourished and strengthened by His Bread of Life.

In the name of Pope Francis, I do not forget to ask you to pray for him, and also for me and all the bishops, that our service to the poorest, from the lowest step on the ladder of God's servants, may convince the world of the proximity of the Kingdom.

Dear friends, may this festive celebration, despite the dramatic circumstances, also be our way of reacting to the forces of evil through the power of love and worship. Christ leads us into His offering of love to the Father for the salvation of the world. Let us embrace His Passion for love; let us welcome His Spirit of truth in this hour of mercy; and let us keep in our hearts the joy of the hope that the communion of the saints maintains in us. Amen!

Chapter 4

Servants of Ecclesial Communion[203]

Each particular Church, a portion of the Catholic Church under the leadership of its Bishop, is also called to missionary conversion. It is the first subject of evangelization, as it is the concrete manifestation of the one Church in one place in the world, and that in it "the Church of Christ, one, holy, catholic and apostolic, is truly present and active."[204]

Dear friends, Pope Francis has taken up this beautiful ecclesiological formulation of the Second Vatican Ecumenical Council in his great programmatic exhortation *Evangelii Gaudium*, to invite the whole Church, but first of all the bishops, to a missionary conversion. This exhortation touches us directly and invites us to look for ways to respond now, given our new mission and the current needs of the Church and the world. The Holy Father adds: "For this missionary impulse to be ever more intense, generous and fruitful, I also exhort each particular Church to enter into a determined process of discernment, purification and reform."[205]

---

[203] Congress for New Bishops, Rome, September 8, 2015.

[204] Second Vatican Council, Decree *Christus Dominus* on the Pastoral Office of Bishops, no. 11; Pope Francis, Apostolic Exhortation *Evangelii Gaudium*, no. 30. Hereafter: EG.

[205] EG, no. 30.

What can this missionary conversion mean for us and for the particular Church to which we are sent? The opening quotation, taken from the Decree *Christus Dominus* on the Pastoral Office of Bishops, presents the Church of Christ as a universal subject present and active in Her concrete manifestations, the particular Churches. It does not speak of the Church in terms of a community or federation of local communities but as a single and universal subject, present and acting in a concrete place. What is our place and role in this Church, which is inseparably universal and particular? "Sometimes," writes Pope Francis, "he [the bishop] will stand in front of us to indicate the way and support the hope of the people; other times he will simply be in the midst of all in a simple and merciful proximity; and in certain circumstances he will have to walk behind the people, to help those who have remained behind and—especially—because the flock itself has a sense of smell to find new paths."[206]

The Holy Father has accustomed us to his original metaphors that accompany his actions and arouse enthusiasm. I recognize in his suggestive description his own way of exercising the Petrine ministry that challenges us: What figure of bishop and pastor do we want to be, and perhaps should we become, at this time of Church reform? This is the great question that dwells within us and that we want to discuss in this initial formation session near the tombs of the Holy Apostles Peter and Paul. We are all familiar with models of bishops we know or who have inspired us in history. I know a Colombian bishop who edified me a lot when I was rector of his major seminary in Manizales. A model bishop by his sense of the Church, his doctrine, and his way of governing: He served in three dioceses and then continued to serve as bishop emeritus in an exemplary manner. At the age of ninety-six, he is celebrating sixty

[206] *EG*, no. 31.

years of episcopacy these days. You may have recognized him as His Eminence José de Jesus Pimiento Rodriguez, Archbishop Emeritus of Manizales, whom Pope Francis has just made a cardinal. He is a great man of the Church whose wisdom and pastoral prudence I salute.

Some bishops see the Church with managerial eyes; they are sensitive to Her structures, organization and performance, considering themselves good administrators, and even moderators of a good consensus between priests and faithful; other bishops see the Church as a people governed by the golden rule of charity, especially towards the poor and the suffering and the marginalized, and they are concerned with community life and social issues, while seeking to be a meaningful presence in the media of communication; other bishops promote, above all, the sanctification of the faithful, sacramental life, popular piety, and priestly and religious vocations, and they see themselves preferably as spiritual leaders. These different ways of exercising episcopal ministry correspond to one or another dimension of the mission received. None of them is alien to the nature of the Church. But a unilateral focus on one or the other can leave essential aspects of the episcopal mission suffering.

I. The Bishop and the Church

I will not go any further with this initial evocation of the episcopal ministry, because to frame our reflection adequately, I believe it is opportune and even necessary to introduce our exchanges and dialogue through a kind of "meditation on the Church," according to a well-known work by Father Henri de Lubac, S.J.[207] A reflection on

[207] Henri de Lubac, *Méditation sur l'Église* (Paris: éd. du Cerf, 1956). The Constitution on the Church *Lumen Gentium* is largely inspired by this masterful and serene work, written at a time when the theologian was going through a period of trial caused by suspicions about his orthodoxy.

the figure of the bishop presupposes a vision of the Church of which he is one of the essential pillars as the successor of the Apostles. The bishop is called to serve the Church of God by exercising the triple function of "priest, doctor, and pastor" according to the specific modality of his episcopal ordination. How he exercises this ministry depends in large part on his view of the Church, a view conditioned by his spirituality, his particular formation, and his previous ministerial experiences. Because of God's call, confirmed by the Church, this gaze must now be extended to the dimensions of the universal Church. What a challenge for a bishop who has just been ordained to go beyond his own geographical, cultural, and even spiritual horizon to assume universal responsibility! What a qualitative leap is required to move from the exercise of a particular ministry to a universal missionary responsibility! Does he not need a powerful grace to open his heart and mind beyond his limits and familiar affiliations?

I know of no better example of missionary conversion than what you are living since your episcopal ordination. For the fullness of the priesthood that you have received by ordination commits you to watch (episcopate) over the unity of the people of God for which you are solidly responsible. This ecclesial responsibility consists, above all, in looking after the communion of the universal and particular Church, which means much more than monitoring the observance of canonical discipline in your diocese. I strongly recommend on this subject an excellent article from *La Civiltà Cattolica* of last June that presents the figure of the bishop according to Pope Francis.[208]

[208] Cf. Diego Fares, "The Figure of the Bishop in Pope Francis," *La Civiltà Cattolica*, II, June 13, 2015, pp. 433-449: "What I wish to emphasize is this particular depth of vigilance with respect to more general vigilance or more precise vigilance. Watching refers more to the care of doctrine and customs, while overseeing alludes rather

To introduce the dialogue on this great question, I therefore propose a meditation on the Church with the help of the ecclesiology of communion from the Second Vatican Council. This ecclesiology of the people of God will reveal the sacramental nature of the Church and Her symbolic figure as the Body and Spouse of Christ; this ecclesiological view will ultimately lead us to the figure of the bishop as "servant of ecclesial communion." In the process, I will formulate some questions aimed at furthering personal reflection and the integration of one's own experience. The initial questions could be: "Church of Jesus Christ, what do you have to say about yourself?" "And we, successors of the Apostles in the third millennium, how do we view the Church?"

A. *The Church, God's people on the move*

The Second Vatican Council is widely recognized as an ecclesiological council. The Constitution on the Church, *Lumen Gentium*, has clarified the sacramental nature of the Church and Her hierarchical constitution, including the historically late dimension of episcopal collegiality; it has also recognized and promoted Her charismatic dimension in the service of communion and mission. The Pastoral Constitution *Gaudium et Spes*, for its part, delineated the anthropological and social vision that clarifies and articulates the role of the Church in today's world, particularly in the face of the major issues of marriage and family; of economic, social, and political life; and of the safeguarding of peace between nations.

The immediate postconciliar period, as we know, experienced turbulence and dubious hermeneutics in certain circles, particularly

---

to ensuring that there is salt and light in hearts. Watching speaks of being alert in the face of imminent danger, overseeing instead speaks of patiently supporting the processes through which the Lord brings forth the salvation of his people" (p. 434).

in the liturgical, ecclesial, and social fields, that do not, however, obscure important advances in ecumenism and interreligious dialogue, as well as in the Church's social doctrine. Fifty years after the conclusion of the Council, we can see that its texts have not aged and that the new missionary breath it has channeled is more than ever at the center of attention.

Everyone remembers Pope Francis's first gesture on the balcony of Saint Peter's in Rome on the evening of his election: his inclination towards God's people to invoke their prayer and invite them to walk together towards the Kingdom. The Pope thus symbolically evoked his vision of the Church as God's people walking at the heart of history, guided by the Word of God and animated by the Holy Spirit. To those who would like to see in it a resurrection of the "spirit of the Council," promoted on the margins of the texts, and a reissue of liberationist ecclesiology, it is necessary to remember how fervently the Holy Father repeats a typical Ignatian expression, "Our Blessed Mother the hierarchical Church," thus rejecting any sociologizing reduction, and integrating his ecclesiology of the people of God into the entire conciliar vision. We will come back to this later.

At the turn of the year 2000, on the occasion of the Great Jubilee, Cardinal Joseph Ratzinger took stock of the reception of conciliar ecclesiology, and timely recalled that it was first interpreted superficially, giving rise to endless discussions on structures, to the detriment of its theological novelty as *people of God* rooted in the mystery of Trinitarian communion.[209] This is reflected in the beautiful formula of the Constitution *Lumen Gentium*, which

---

[209] Joseph Ratzinger, *L'ecclesiologia della Costituzione Lumen Gentium*, in the Central Committee of the Great Jubilee of the Year 2000, *Il Concilio Vaticano II: Recezione e attualità allaluce del Giubileo*, pp. 66-81, at p. 75.

concludes the description of the mission of the Holy Spirit in the Church: "Thus the universal Church appears as 'a people gathered in the unity of the Father, the Son and the Holy Spirit.'"[210] Conciliar ecclesiology is founded on God, and then, strongly recalling the future Benedict XVI, it must be interpreted theologically if we want to avoid the ideological manipulations that allow the ecclesial community to dominant cultural models.

One of the major turning points in conciliar ecclesiology in the chapter on the people of God is to have treated first of all the common priesthood of the faithful as the foundation of the dignity of the people of God:

> The Lord Christ, High Priest taken from among men (cf. Heb 5:1-5) made the new people "a kingdom of priests for God his Father" (Rev 1:6; 5:9-10). Indeed, through the regeneration and anointing of the Holy Spirit, the baptized are consecrated to be a spiritual house and a holy priesthood, in order to offer spiritual sacrifices, through all the works of the Christian, and to proclaim the praises of the One who called them from darkness to his wonderful light (cf. 1 Pet 2:4-11).[211]

This editorial choice has restored and highlighted the fundamental dignity of the "royal priesthood" in the people of God, without diminishing the specificity of the hierarchical or ministerial priesthood. The Council also stressed that the two priesthoods are correlative and complementary, since both "participate, each in its own way, in the one priesthood of Christ."[212]

---

[210]LG, no. 4; see Saint Cyprian, *De Orat. Dom.* 23, PL 4, 553; Hartel, III A, 285; Saint Augustinus, *Serm.* 71, 20, 33, PL 38, 463ff; Saint John Damascene, *Adv. Iconoel.* 12, PG 96, 1358 D.

[211]LG, no. 10.

[212]Ibid.

Friends of the Bridegroom

It is important for the bishop to be able to contemplate the priestly identity of his people because the episcopal, priestly, and diaconal ministry exists for the conscious and fruitful exercise of this "royal priesthood." Such a view is essential to the unity of the particular Church and to the missionary influence of the Christian communities. These are all the more alive and missionary because communion between pastors and the faithful is founded on the same priestly dignity and lived as an exchange of gifts "both hierarchical and charismatic,"[213] which the Spirit provides to the Church in order to beautify it, rejuvenate it, and lead it "to perfect union with its Spouse."[214]

What are the fruits of a harmonious mutual relationship between the two essentially different and complementary participations of the priesthood of Christ? Unless foreign factors interfere, we see an abundance of charisms that the Holy Spirit pours into the people of God, inspiring vocations to the priesthood and to consecrated life, united and fruitful homes, personal and community testimonies of ecumenical openness and commitment to justice, social peace, and the safeguarding of creation. If this communion is lacking, the ground is conducive to the development of secularization, sectarianism, and religious indifference. On the other hand, where the two forms of Christ's one priesthood are mutually fruitful, the Church evangelizes "by attraction,"[215] through "the reception of the sacraments, prayer and thanksgiving, the witness of a holy life, abnegation and active charity."[216]

In environments where a mentality of power, rivalries and ideological division prevails, there is a decline in Christian joy, an anaemic or sterile pastoral care, sometimes accompanied by

[213]LG, no. 4.
[214]Ibid.
[215]EG, no. 14.
[216]LG, no. 10.

destructive media campaigns. Pope Francis constantly denounces spiritual mundanity, or worldliness at all, that undermines the credibility of the Church and Her pastors. It is then necessary for an authentic conversion of his ministers to the humility and merciful compassion of the Lord to rekindle hope in the baptized and to help communities to walk together again in a spirit of conversion and reconciliation. The ecclesiology of the people of God that Francis lives and teaches is essentially missionary and profoundly theological; it "has its roots in the Trinity"[217] and is built on "the primacy of grace."[218] "To be Church," he writes, "is to be the People of God, in accordance with the Father's great plan of love. This calls us to be the leaven of God in humanity."[219] What spiritual and pastoral demands do they make on us bishops, who walk with the people of God "among the persecutions of the world and the consolations of God."[220]

B. Sacrament of Trinitarian communion

At the beginning, we mentioned the challenge of moving from a priestly mission in the service of a diocese to an episcopal mission in the service of the universal Church. The broadening of the view that this implies has a geographical dimension, because of the status of members of the episcopal college co-responsible for the universal Church; but it also has a sacramental dimension, rooted in the mystery of ecclesial communion, of which the bishop is a major articulation. The Dogmatic Constitution *Lumen Gentium* puts into play from the very beginning the notion of sacrament that specifies the profound nature of the Church and thus renews Her relationship to the world:

[217]*EG*, no. 111.
[218]*EG*, no. 112
[219]*EG*, no. 114.
[220]*LG*, no. 8.

Friends of the Bridegroom

The Holy Council gathered in the Holy Spirit ardently desires to illuminate all men with the light of Christ who shines on the face of the Church.... This, for its part, is in Christ as a sacrament, or if you will, as a sign and a means of operating intimate union with God and the unity of the whole human race.[221]

We see here the notion of sacrament as an "effective sign of grace" converging with the notion of "communion" (*koinonia*),[222] which are combined in "a complex reality formed by a human element and a divine element."[223]

The notion of sacrament is applied to the Church, the Body of Christ, with the help of the analogy of the Incarnate Word: "Just as the nature assumed by the divine Word serves it as an instrument of salvation, a living instrument indissolubly united to himself, so this ecclesial organism serves the Spirit of Christ who gives it life for the growth of the body (cf. Eph 4:16)."[224]

The notion of communion is applied in a very nuanced and circumspect way, to mark the way to ecumenism without sacrificing the proper vision of Catholic truth: "This Church, constituted and organized in this world as a community, subsists in the Catholic Church, governed by the successor of Peter and the bishops in communion with him."[225] This is essentially the affirmation of the identity of the Catholic Church expressed in such a way as not to exclude other ecclesial realities. The Council adds: "Even though, outside this whole, there are several elements of sanctification

---

[221] LG, no. 1.
[222] See Jean-Marie Tillard, "Communion," in J.-Y. Lacoste, ed., *Dictionnaire critique de théologie*, pp. 285-293.
[223] LG, no. 8.
[224] Ibid.
[225] Ibid.

and truth which, as gifts proper to the Church of Christ, call for Catholic unity."[226]

The Church offers the light of Christ to the world through the proclamation of the Word of God and the sacraments that structure Her participation in Trinitarian communion. This sacramental communion is nourished, above all, by the paschal sacrifice of Christ, which transcends and crosses the centuries, diachronically and synchronically, conveyed by communities guided by the communion of the successors of the Apostles *cum and sub Petro*. This participation in Trinitarian communion derives first of all from the sacraments of Christian initiation, and it is prolonged and consolidated by the other sacraments, as well as by the variety of charisms that contribute to the unity of the Church and Her missionary dynamism.

In concrete terms, the grace of Baptism confers on the child of God his or her filial identity; the grace of Confirmation reinforces this filial identity for witness by the seal of the Holy Spirit; the grace of the Eucharist gathers the children of God around the sacrificial offering of Christ to the Father, obtaining for them the bestowal of the Holy Spirit on the assembly and on all creation.

This Trinitarian structure of Christian initiation is prolonged and perfected by the other sacraments, each of which contributes in its own way to the building up of the Church, the Body of Christ. The Sacrament of Marriage confers on the human couple, created in the image of God, a resemblance to Trinitarian love, which transforms the family into an ecclesial reality, like an icon of the Holy Trinity. Christ the Lord "comes to meet the spouses through the Sacrament of Marriage" and "dwells with them."[227] He makes His own the relationship of love and the community of life between

---

[226]Ibid.

[227]Second Vatican Council, Pastoral Constitution on the Church in the Modern World *Gaudium et Spes*, no. 48, §2.

man and woman, expressing in it truly and not only symbolically His own love for the Church, His Bride, thus conferring on the family institution an authentic ecclesial mission.

Moreover, the two different and complementary contributions of the one priesthood of Christ have been the subject of much ink for decades, either to justify or criticize this firm doctrine of the Catholic Church. Here, as in other areas, a Trinitarian deepening makes it possible to resolve unhealthy tensions and to overcome any rivalry between clerics and laity. The Council clearly affirms the essential difference, and not only in degrees, between the two priests, but it leaves it to the theologians to provide an explanation.

I believe, for my part, that the common or royal priesthood of the baptized resides in the participation in the priesthood of the Son inasmuch as He offers Himself in sacrifice to the Father for us, in Love, and in return obtains for us the gift of the Holy Spirit. As for the ministerial or apostolic priesthood, I see it as essentially different and founded on the fact that Christ is the Envoy of the Father; He represents the Father, speaking with His authority and obeying Him in everything. In a way, He is "the Apostle of the Father," this apostolic dimension being added to and completing His filial priesthood. This "apostolic" dimension of His one priesthood becomes more visible in the economy of salvation on the evening of Easter, when the risen Lord appears to the Apostles, blows the Holy Spirit on them, and thus confers on them the power to forgive sins in the name of the three divine Persons.

It follows from this that the Apostles and their successors are thus endowed and sent by Him to prolong His "apostolic" or "ministerial" priesthood. Hence their reference to the figure of the Father and their experience of spiritual fatherhood specific to bishops and, to a lesser extent, to priests. From this Trinitarian perspective, which is also explicitly mentioned in the Post-Synodal Apostolic Exhortation

Pastores Gregis,[228] there emerges a more obvious articulation of the ordination of hierarchical ministers to the promotion of the royal (filial) priesthood of the baptized. In this light, any rivalry or conflict between the members of the two priesthoods appears contrary to the Spirit of Christ. For the latter confirms their unity and their mutual fertilization in the life of the Church, as he confirms the unity of the Father and the Son in the Trinity. Just as the Father and the Son co-exist in the Spirit of Their eternal Love, so pastors and faithful build each other up through their mutual love, enriched by their blessed priestly difference and complementarity.

The Church, the people of God, therefore, participates in the communion of the divine Persons through the grace of Baptism and through all the sacramental articulations that make Her "a sign and a means of operating intimate union with God and the unity of the whole human race."[229] In this way, She carries out Her mission through the exercise of the priesthood of Jesus Christ, Who spreads Trinitarian Love throughout the world. Through the proclamation of the Gospel and the celebration of the sacraments of Christian initiation, and through their extension into Her hierarchical and charismatic structure, the Church of Christ, founded and inhabited by Trinitarian Love, thus becomes ever more missionary, a "sign and instrument" of communion, pure service to the Love of Christ — in short, *Sacramentum Trinitatis*.

How is the sacramentality of the Church integrated into our ecclesiological visions? What impact does it have or should it have

---

[228] Saint John Paul II, Post-Synodal Apostolic Exhortation *Pastores Gregis*, no. 7: "Christ is the original icon of the Father and the manifestation of his merciful presence among men. The Bishop, acting in the person and in the name of Christ himself, becomes, in the Church entrusted to him, a living sign of the Lord Jesus, Pastor and Spouse, Master and Pontiff of the Church."

[229] *LG*, no. 1.

on the exercise of episcopal ministry? Is our ecclesiology of communion fundamentally Eucharistic? What is its relationship to episcopal collegiality and ecumenism?

C. *"Our Blessed Mother the Hierarchical Church"*

Our view of the Church has so far embraced Her sociological visibility as the people of God on the march and Her Trinitarian and Eucharistic dimensions, hidden under the notion of communion, of a sacramental significance. We are now continuing our contemplation of the light of Christ shining on the face of the Church, in order to reflect it as much as possible for our contemporaries. The previous developments reveal it in part but do not exhaust its richness. The Council was careful to enumerate various biblical images that prevent us from avoiding any worldly reduction of the mystery of the Church. I would like to mention one that deserves our attention because of its suggestive and unusual character. I am thinking of the Ignatian expression that often comes forth from the mouth of Pope Francis, "Our Blessed Mother the Hierarchical Church."

The expression is rather paradoxical and at first glance seems outdated or as belonging to another age because this synthetic expression unites two dimensions that seem at first sight to be mutually exclusive: on the one hand, the maternity of the Church, and on the other hand, Her hierarchical structure. The first reminds us of the Virgin Mary and the second of the bishops. How can they be integrated into a balanced ecclesiological vision?

Francis responded with the help of Hans Urs von Balthasar, ranking like him what he called the Marian principle and the Petrine principle of the Church.[230] "In the Church, Mary is more

---

[230]Cf. H. Urs von Balthasar, *Le Complexe antiromain: Essai sur les structures ecclésiales* (Paris: Apostolat des éditions, 1976), chap. 5, "L'amour maternel enveloppant de l'Église," pp. 191-235.

fundamental than Peter," they both affirm, for Mary embodies the immaculate faith by which the Church welcomes and gives to the world the incarnate Word. In the most important hierarchy, that of faith and love, Mary reigns first, her fecundity conferring on her a universal maternity that envelops in her great mantle all the members of the Body of Christ. Peter represents the ministry in the Church; he is the principle of his visible unity as a universal pastor as Bishop of Rome and head of the Episcopal College. He can exercise his ministry of representing Christ as Head and Spouse of the Church, because the Church, Body and Bride of Christ, is already constituted by the immaculate faith of Mary. Let us listen in this regard to an echo of the Council:

> The Church is even called "the Jerusalem from above" and "our mother" (Gal 4:26; Rev. 12:17); she appears as the immaculate wife of the Lamb without spot (Rev. 19:7; 21:2, 9; 22:17). This bride, Christ "loved her ... and gave himself for her, in order to sanctify her" (Eph 5:25-26); he associated himself with her by an indissoluble and unceasing pact; "he nourishes and cares for her" (Eph 5:29), and he wanted her, after purifying her, to be united and submissive to him in love and faithfulness (cf. Eph 5:24).[231]

To deepen our meditation on the Church, I draw attention to this nuptial symbolism that runs through the entire Bible, from Genesis to Revelation, with the Song of Songs at the center as the hermeneutical key to the relationship between God and His people, between Christ and the Church. Ecclesiology has not yet fully integrated this symbolism, which makes it possible to highlight from another point of view the unity and personality of the Church. A profound look at the Church, Wife and Mother, in the

[231]LG, no. 6.

light of pneumatology and Mariology, can refine and even transform the relationships between Her members, especially between the bishop and his faithful.

Let us recall in passing that the greatest conciliar debate was on how to consider the Virgin Mary in relation to the Church. Should we prefer a separate document to highlight her preeminent figure, or should we prefer a chapter within the Constitution on the Church? The debate was dramatic, and the result very close, because the conciliar assembly was really divided between two widely represented tendencies. The second opinion prevailed, thanks to God, thus curbing the exaltation of Mary's privileges above the Church, and reintegrating her as a member, "the most excellent," but a member nevertheless, as a model and realization typical of the Church. In this way, the conciliar ecclesiology has been enriched by a very dense Marian chapter without being exhaustive, crowning a harmonious overall vision, even if it has remained too discreet under the profile of nuptiality and motherhood. The pontificate of Saint John Paul II, lived under the sign of Mary at the foot of the Cross, confirmed the hermeneutics of the Council that Paul VI wanted to balance on the last day by declaring the Virgin Mary to be Mother of the Church. Hence the relevance of Francis's ecclesiological formula, "Our Blessed Mother the Hierarchical Church," which encourages us to look at the Church as a person, a subject, and not only as an organization, a people, a communion, but especially as a Bride and a Mother, "a mystical Person," according to the formula of Saint Thomas Aquinas.[232]

What importance can this bridal look have for a pastor who wants to be ahead of, in the middle of, and even sometimes behind

---

[232] Saint Thomas Aquinas, *In Col.* 1, lesson 6: "Christ and the Church are one mystical person, whose head is Christ, and whose body [is] all the righteous."

his flock? Is it not enough for him to have a good devotion to the Virgin Mary and to invoke her often in the face of the challenges of the pastoral task? If the pastor sees Mary exclusively as a model or mediator in Heaven, and if he does not see her discreet and active presence among the people of God, how will he integrate the popular piety that reveals Mary's preferential option for the poor? Moreover, if the principle of unity of the Church represented by Peter as head of the college of bishops is not understood within the principle of unity represented by Mary as the intimate form of ecclesial communion, what kind of ecclesial communion will be promoted, and with what means? Are there not legal and disciplinary aspects that risk supplanting the pastoral attitude and the mystagogical dimension? And what about ecumenism with the Orthodox?

The bishop's view of the Church is reflected in all his personal and community relationships, both locally and universally. Depending on the depth of his gaze, he will have a different way of establishing his pastoral priorities and living the vertical and horizontal communion of the universal Church in his particular Church. If he takes up the word of Jesus to his beloved disciple at the foot of the Cross, he will welcome the Mother of the Savior as his mother, the new Eve, the Bride of the sacrificed and victorious Lamb. Is not her apostolic fruitfulness multiplied in the very measure of her union with this immaculate Virgin, Mother of the Church? In short, just as the Church is not a mother without being a wife, can pastors really be paternal without a husband's view of the Church?

II. The Bishop, servant of ecclesial communion

Our meditation on the Church began with an evocation of the particular Church, the first subject of evangelization, in which the Church of Jesus Christ, one, holy, catholic, and apostolic, is present and active. Having contemplated Her mystery in the reality of God's people and having clarified Her sacramental nature as a communion of persons participating in the communion of divine Persons, we now return to the figure of the bishop, who is the link between the universal Church and the particular Church.

Whether planted in Rome, Jerusalem, Montevideo, Sydney, or Kampala, the Church is always at the same time universal and particular, this double dimension characterizing Her as a mystery of communion in missionary tension towards union with God and the unity of all humanity.

The bishop, to whom a particular Church is entrusted, must ensure that the universality of the Church in his particular Church, and the particularity of his Church in the universal Church, are safeguarded. Both dimensions are essential, and the bishop, by virtue of his membership in the episcopal college, is the concrete link that binds them together in a sacramental way. Consequently, the bishop cannot limit himself to taking care of the concrete flock of which he is the pastor. He must feel co-responsible for the universal Church, and therefore for all the other particular Churches entrusted to his colleagues in the Episcopal College. The exercise of this responsibility obviously involves precise guidelines and conditions that are determined by canon law. But the essential thing remains his ecclesiological vision, his adherence to the Pontifical Magisterium, his participation in the effective or affective expressions of episcopal collegiality, his interest in the missionary conversion required of each particular Church.

"Servant of ecclesial communion," therefore, means for the bishop to be aware of the universal nature of the Church, at Whose service he animates his particular community, so that it may live in this openness, and not close itself to its own geographical, ethnic, or cultural horizon. The health of a particular Church shines through Her contribution to the universal communion of the Church; this contribution obviously includes Her participation in papal charities, but it is above all of a qualitative nature, through the holiness of Her members, their missionary dynamism, and their witness to unity.

The bishop is the principle of unity that guarantees the communion and mission of a particular Church, but he is also the essential link of communion between that Church and all the other particular Churches of the past or present, since the communion of the Church embraces both the continuity of generations in Tradition and the present solidarity of all the particular Churches *cum et sub Petro.*

It is remarkable to note that the council Decree *Christus Dominus,* on the Pastoral Office of Bishops, deals first and foremost with the responsibility of the bishop towards the universal Church as a member of the Episcopal College, before dealing with his pastoral responsibility towards a particular Church. "Servants of ecclesial communion," therefore, presupposes in bishops a deep awareness of their own sacramental mystery, which unites them as members of the college of the successors of the Apostles, thus becoming co-responsible collegially for the universal Church, even if their pastoral activity attaches them especially to the service of the particular Church entrusted to their care.

With regard to his own portion of the universal Church, the bishop is the pastor "with the help of his presbytery." The absolute priority will therefore be the unity of this presbytery, for the fruitful service of the royal priesthood of the baptized requires a witness of unity that makes the presence of the risen Lord more credible in the ecclesial community and among its pastors.

This witness certainly depends on the goodwill of all and on their sincere search for holiness. It will increasingly rely on the Golden Rule of mutual love in the Spirit of Jesus, but it would be greatly favored by a theology of vocation and states of life, which shows their complementary and harmonious relationship within the framework of a Trinitarian ecclesiology.[233]

In this context, the universal call to holiness is realized as the perfection of charity in all states of life. Contemplated as a participation in the Trinitarian Love, this perfection of charity favors the mutual fecundation of vocations to the priesthood and to consecrated life, in the service of the first and most fragile cell of the Church, the family.[234] The bishop, servant of ecclesial communion, fixing his gaze on Christ, and the Church, His Bride, will not fail to promote the communion of all states of life in the service of the family, the Domestic Church, which is called more than ever to radiate the light of Christ in a confused world.

Conclusion

Dear friends, at the invitation of the Holy Father, we have the grace to begin our episcopal ministry with an experience of sacramental fraternity in Rome near the tombs of Saints Peter and Paul, at the dawn of the Great Jubilee of Mercy. The episcopal ordination and the pastoral mission you have received certainly arouse in you feelings of gratitude, but also a salutary fear in the face of the responsibility and missionary conversion they imply. Hence, we feel the increased demand for prayer, accompanied by an instinctive and daily supplication to the Holy Spirit so that He

---

[233] I highly recommend the work of H. Urs von Balthasar on this point: *Christlicher Stand* (Johannes Verlag, 1977). In English, *The Christian State of Life* (Ignatius Press, 2002); in Italian, *Gli stati di vita del cristiano*, 2nd ed. (Jaca Book, 1996); in French, *L'état de vie chrétien*, translated from German, by J. de Vulpillières (Einsiedeln: Johannes Verlag, 2016). It is a complete and systematic theology of the different forms of vocation, which responds to the current needs of an attractive and demanding evangelical vision.

[234] H. Urs von Balthasar, op. cit., Italian version, pp. 330-335.

may work in us to open our hearts and minds to the universal and particular dimensions of our episcopal mission.

Whatever our talents and previous experiences, the service of ecclesial communion that is required of us exceeds our capacities and presupposes on our part a daily vigilance so that we are pastors attentive to the needs of God's people, contemplatives of the Trinitarian mystery that appears in ecclesial communion, and friends of the Bridegroom inhabited by Jesus' gaze upon the Church, His Bride. Episcopal ordination expropriated us from ourselves to belong totally to Him, but this grace must also be acquired through spiritual and missionary conversion. For, in order to walk ahead, in the midst of and behind the people entrusted to us, we must closely follow the One Shepherd and faithfully watch with Him over the unity of the universal and particular Church for which we are solidly responsible.

Pope Francis shows us the way to a missionary conversion that relaunches evangelization "by attraction."[235] Let us allow ourselves to be touched by his testimony and seek, like him, to serve the Trinitarian communion that shines on the face of the Church. As bishops of the one, holy, catholic, and apostolic Church, in the particular portion entrusted to us, let us ask for the grace to follow Christ the Lord with dignity, in profound communion with the Successor of Peter and all our confreres, so that the world may believe that God has given it His only Son and eternal Life.

[235] EG, no. 14.

Part 2

Priestly Celibacy in the Light of Mary

When Jesus saw his mother and the disciple there whom he loved, he said to his mother, "Woman, behold, your son." Then he said to the disciple, "Behold, your mother." And from that hour the disciple took her into his home.

—John 19:26–27

Chapter 5

Upper Room: Invocation of the Holy Spirit with Mary in Fraternal Communion[236]

When they entered the city they went to the upper room where they were staying, Peter and John and James and Andrew, Philip and Thomas, Bartholomew and Matthew, James son of Alphaeus, Simon the Zealot, and Judas son of James. All these devoted themselves with one accord to prayer, together with some women, and Mary the mother of Jesus, and his brothers.[237]

Pope John Paul II cherished this scene from the Acts of the Apostles. He literally immersed himself in it through contemplation, conscious of belonging to this mystery with the whole Church and especially with priests. From the Upper Room in Jerusalem, he addressed this message to the priests:

From this Holy Hall, I spontaneously imagine you in the most diverse parts of the world, with your thousand faces, the youngest and the oldest, in your different states of mind, reflecting for many, thanks to God, joy and enthusiasm; for others, perhaps, suffering, weariness, distress. In all of you, I

---

[236] Rome, Basilica of Saint Paul Outside the Walls, June 10, 2010.
[237] Acts 1:13-14.

come to honour the image of Christ that you have received through consecration, this "character" that marks each of you in an indelible way. It is the sign of the love of predilection that touches every priest and on which he can always count to move forward with joy, or to start again with a new enthusiasm, in the perspective of ever greater fidelity.[238]

This message from the cenacle of Jerusalem, the holy city *par excellence*, challenges us in this basilica and in this blessed hour of the Year for Priests. It reminds us of the love of predilection that has chosen us and that brings us together in prayer at the cenacle, just as the Apostles were in prayer with Mary after the Resurrection, waiting for the fulfillment of the Lord's promise: "You will receive a strength, that of the Holy Spirit, that will come upon you. Then you will be my witnesses in Jerusalem, in all Judea and Samaria, and to the ends of the earth."[239]

Saint Irenaeus of Lyon describes this power of the Spirit, Who has traversed the centuries:

The Spirit of God descended upon the Lord, the Spirit of wisdom and intelligence, the Spirit of counsel and strength, the Spirit of knowledge and piety, the Spirit of fear of God. In turn, the Lord gave it to the Church, sending the Paraclete from Heaven over the whole earth, where the devil was struck down like lightning, says the Lord.[240]

On the day of my priestly ordination, after the laying on of hands, I was touched by a word of Saint Paul for the rest of my

---

[238] Saint John Paul II, *Letter to Priests*, Holy Thursday of the Year 2000, no. 3.

[239] Acts 1:8.

[240] Saint Irenaeus, *Contre les hérésies*, 1, 10, 1-3, *Sources chrétiennes* 210 (Paris: éd. du Cerf, 1974), p. 328.

days: "Not that I have already reached the goal, nor have I already become perfect; but I continue my journey to try to grasp, having been grasped myself by Christ Jesus."[241] Ordained a priest in May 1968, I began my ministry in an atmosphere of generalized protest that could have caused me to deviate or even interrupt my journey, as was the case for many priests and religious at that time. The missionary experience, priestly friendship, and the proximity of the poor helped me to survive the turbulence of the postconciliar years.

Today we are witnessing an unprecedented wave of protest against the Church and the priesthood, following the unveiling of scandals, the gravity of which we must acknowledge and sincerely correct. But beyond the necessary purifications deserved by our sins, we must also recognize at this time an open opposition to our service of truth, and attacks from outside and even from within to divide the Church. We pray together for the unity of the Church and for the sanctification of priests, these heralds of the Good News of salvation.

In the authentic Spirit of the Second Vatican Council, we listen to the Word of God, as the conciliar fathers who gave us the Constitution *Dei Verbum*:

> We proclaim to you eternal life, which was with the Father and which appeared to us: what we have seen and heard, we proclaim to you, so that you too may be in communion with us, and our communion may be with the Father and with his Son. Jesus Christ.[242]

Dear friends, a great priestly figure accompanies us and guides us in this meditation, the holy Curé d'Ars, patron saint of all priests, by the grace of God and the wisdom of the Church.

---

[241] Phil 3:12.
[242] 1 Jn 1:2-3.

Friends of the Bridegroom

Saint Jean-Marie Vianney confessed France, repentant, torn, and wounded by the Revolution and its aftermath. He was an exemplary priest and a zealous pastor. He restored prayer to the heart of the priestly life. "We had deserved not to pray, but God, in his kindness, allowed us to talk to him. Our prayer is an incense that he receives with extreme pleasure."[243] "O my God, if my tongue cannot say at all times that I love you, at least I want my heart to repeat it to you as many times as I breathe."

We are many in this basilica with Mary, the Mother of Jesus and our Mother. Together, "we worship the Father in Spirit and truth through the mediation of the Son who brings heavenly blessings upon the world from the Father."[244] By faith we are united with all the priests of the world in fraternal communion under the leadership of our Holy Father Pope Benedict XVI, whom we thank from the bottom of our hearts for the declaration of this Year for Priests.

I. The mystery of the priesthood

The Catholic Church today has 408,024 priests spread over five continents. Four hundred thousand priests is a lot—and a small number for more than a billion Catholics. We have 400,000 priests, and yet there is only one Priest, Christ Jesus, the only Mediator of the New Covenant, the One Who presented, "with a loud cry and tears, his prayer and supplication to God who could save him from death; and, because he submitted himself in everything, he was heard."[245]

Because of his disobedience, sinful man has lost from the beginning the grace of divine filiation. This is why men are born

[243] Alfred Monnin, *L'esprit du curé d'Ars dans ses catéchismes* (Paris: Téqui, 2007).
[244] Saint Cyril of Alexandria, *Commentary on the Second Letter to the Corinthians* (Oxford: ed. P.E. Pusey, 1872), 3, pp. 352-354.
[245] Heb 5:7.

deprived of original grace. This grace had to be restored by the obedience of Jesus Christ:

> Even though he is the Son, he nevertheless learned obedience by the sufferings of his Passion; and thus, led to his perfection, he became for all those who obey him the cause of eternal salvation. For God has proclaimed him high priest according to the priesthood of Melchizedek.[246]

This unique High Priest stands on Mount Calvary as a new Moses, supporting the struggle of the forces of love against the forces of evil. With His arms nailed to the Cross of our churches, but with His eyes open like the crucifix of San Damiano, He speaks about the Church, the world, and the cosmos, the great epiclesis.

In each Eucharist, the immense epiclesis of Pentecost hears and crowns the supplication of the Cross. Christ, with His arms stretched out between Heaven and earth, gathers all the miseries and intentions of the world. He transforms all the world's pain, refusals, and hopes into a pleasant offering. In a single act of Infinite Love, He presents to the Father the work of men, the sufferings of humanity, and the goods of the cosmos. In Him, "all is accomplished." For the sacrifice of the Son's love satisfies all the love requirements of the New Covenant. His descent into Hell to the depths of the night makes the Word of God, the Word of the Father, resound to the limits of the universe, proclaiming: "You are my beloved Son; in you I have put all my love."[247]

The Father thus answers the Son's prayer: "Father, glorify me with you with the glory that I had with you before the world was."[248] Unable to refuse anything to His Son, the Father sends down upon

[246] Heb 5:8-10.
[247] Mk 1:11.
[248] Jn 17:5.

Him the ultimate gift of glory, the gift of the Holy Spirit, according to the word of Saint John the Evangelist and the interpretation of Saint Gregory of Nyssa.

Hence the Gospel of God proclaimed by Paul to the Romans, which "concerns his Son, born according to the flesh of the lineage of David, established, according to the Holy Spirit, Son of God with power through his resurrection from the dead, Jesus Christ our Lord."[249] The Resurrection of Christ is the supreme revelation of the mystery of the Father, the confirmation of the glory of the Son, and the foundation of creation and salvation.

The Church of God has carried this Gospel of God to the whole world since its origins, in the power of the Holy Spirit. We are witnessing it.

Dear brother priests, the Church is the Sacrament of Salvation. In the Church, we are the sacrament of this High Priest of present and future goods. We were born from the exchange of love between the divine Persons, and Christ the Priest placed His heavenly and glorious imprint on us. Inhabited and possessed by Him, let us raise to God the Father the supplication and cry of suffering humanity. Gathered together by Him, with Him and in Him, in communion with the people of God, let us recognize our own mystery and give thanks to God.

Four hundred thousand priests and yet only one Priest. By the power of the Holy Spirit, the risen One is joined by the ministers of His Word and offering. Through us, He remains present as He was on the first day — and even more than on the first day, because He promised that we would do things greater than He.[250] Christ went to meet His brothers and sisters as He walked towards the Cross. We, His ministers, go to our brothers and sisters in His name and

[249]Rom 1:3-4.
[250]Cf. Jn 14:12.

in His power as risen Lord. We are seized by Christ, the fullness of the Word, and sent on all the roads of the world on the wings of the Spirit.

"That is why," writes Benedict XVI, "the priest who acts *in persona Christi Capitis* and in representation of the Lord, never acts in the name of an absent person, but in the very Person of the risen Christ, who makes himself present through his truly concrete action."[251]

The Holy Spirit guarantees our unity of being and action with the one Priest, we who are 400,000. He is the single Shepherd who turns the multitude into a single flock. For if the sacrament of the priesthood is multiplied, the mystery of the priesthood remains unique and the same, just as the consecrated hosts are multiple, but the Body of the Son of God present in them is unique and the same.

Benedict XVI draws spiritual and pastoral consequences from this unity:

> For the priest is worth what Christ said of himself: "My teaching is not mine" (Jn 7:16); that is, Christ does not propose himself, but, as Son, he is the voice, the word of the Father. The priest must also always speak and act like this: "My doctrine is not mine, I do not spread my ideas or what I like, but I am the mouth and heart of Christ and I make present this unique and common doctrine, which created the universal Church and which creates eternal life."[252]

May we, dear friends, keep a keen awareness of acting *in persona Christi*, in the unity of the Person of Christ. Without this, the food we offer to the faithful loses the taste of mystery, and the salt of our priestly life fades. May our lives keep the flavor of the mystery, and,

---

[251] Benedict XVI, General Audience, Wednesday, April 14, 2010.
[252] Ibid.

for this reason, may they be, above all, a friendship with Christ: "Do you love me, Peter? Feed my sheep."[253] Lived in this love, the priest's mission of feeding the sheep will then be fulfilled in the Spirit of the Lord and in unity with Peter's successor.

II. The Holy Spirit, the Virgin Mary, and the Church

Let us now seek the secret and unknown foundation of priestly holiness where all the mysteries of the priesthood converge: in the spiritual intimacy of the Mother and the Son where the Spirit of God reigns.

On the waters of the primordial creation, the Spirit hovers and brings forth order and life. The psalmist echoes this wonder by singing: "O Lord our God, how great is your name in the whole universe."[254] Throughout the history of salvation, the Spirit stands upon the patriarchs and prophets, gathering the chosen people around the Promise and the "Ten Words" of the Covenant. The prophet Isaiah echoes this holy story: "How beautiful are the steps of the bearers of good news on the mountains!"[255]

In the Nazareth chamber, the Spirit covers the Virgin with His shadow so that she can give birth to the Messiah. She consents with all her being: "May it happen to me according to your word."[256] She then accompanies the Incarnate Word throughout His earthly life; she walks with Him in faith, often without understanding, constantly broadening the unconditional and boundless yes that she had given once and for all to the angel of the Annunciation.

At the foot of the Cross, she stands silent, consenting without understanding to the death of her Son, communicating painfully to the death of the Word of life she had given birth to.

[253] Jn 21:15.
[254] Ps 8:2.
[255] Is 52:7.
[256] Lk 1:38.

The Spirit holds her in this "nuptial" yes that marries the destiny of the sacrificed Lamb. The Virgin of Sorrows is the Bride of the Lamb. In her and through her, the whole Church is associated with the sacrifice of the Redeemer. In her and through her, in the unity of the Spirit, the whole Church is baptized into the death of Christ and participates in His Resurrection.

So here we are with her in the Cenacle, priests of the New Covenant, born of her spiritual motherhood, and animated by faith in the victory of the Word over death and Hell. Here we are, imploring with one heart with Christ for the coming of the Kingdom of God, the revelation of the sons of God and the glorification of all things in God.[257]

Our priestly holiness in and with Christ is enveloped in the unity of the Mother and the Son, in the indissoluble union of the sacrificed Lamb and the Bride of the Lamb. Let us not forget that the redemptive blood of the High Priest comes from the immaculate womb of Mary, who gave Him life and who offered herself with Him. This is why this very pure blood purifies us, this blood of Christ "who, through the eternal spirit, offered himself to God as a spotless victim."[258]

"All the good works together," wrote the Curé d'Ars, "do not amount to the sacrifice of the Mass, because they are the works of men, and the holy Mass is the work of God. Martyrdom is nothing compared to anything else: it is the sacrifice that man makes to God of his life; Mass is the sacrifice that God makes for man of his Body and Blood."[259]

The greatness and holiness of the priest come from this divine work. It is not a human work that we offer to God; it is God

[257] Cf. Rom 8:19ff.
[258] Heb 9:14.
[259] A. Monnin, *L'esprit du Curé d'Ars*, p. 108.

that we offer to God. "How is this possible?" we could ask with Mary, echoing her question to the angel. "Nothing is impossible for God"[260] was the answer given to the Virgin with the tangible sign of Elizabeth's fertility. Let us welcome and make our own this response, with Mary, so that "our life may no longer be ours, but his who died and rose again for us."[261] "Nothing is impossible for God." The Gospel tells us elsewhere: "Everything is possible to the one who believes."[262]

"Priests have a special covenant with the Most Holy Mother of God," writes Saint John Eudes.

> As the Eternal Father made her a participant in his divine paternity, so he gives priests to form this same Jesus in the Holy Eucharist and in the hearts of the faithful. As the Son made her his cooperator in the work of the redemption of the world, so priests are his cooperators in the work of the salvation of souls. As the Holy Spirit associated her in the masterpiece that is the mystery of the Incarnation, so he associates the priests with him for a continuation of this mystery in every Christian through baptism.[263]

Virgin Mary, *Mater misericordiae, vita dulcedo et spes nostra, salve!* In your holy company, Mother of Mercy, we drink from the source of love. Our thirsty hearts and worried souls reach through you to the bridal enclosure of the New Covenant. "This is why priests, having such a close covenant and such wonderful conformity with the Mother of the High Priest," adds Saint John Eudes, "have very

---

[260] Lk 1:37.
[261] Eucharistic Prayer IV.
[262] Mk 9:23.
[263] Saint John Eudes, *Manuel pour l'usage d'une Communauté Ecclésiastique*, Œuvre Complète III (Paris: Gabriel Beauchesne et Cie, 1906), LXIX, p. 216.

special obligations to love her, to honor her, and to clothe themselves with her virtues and dispositions. Enter into the desire to strive for it with all your heart. Offer yourself to her and ask her to help you strongly."[264]

III. Epiclesis upon the world

"If you knew the gift of God and who is the one who tells you: 'Give me something to drink,' you would have asked and he would have given you living water."[265] The Spirit of the Lord is living water, a vital breath, but He is also an impetuous wind that shakes the house, a joyful dove that brings peace, a fire that sets it aflame, a light that pierces darkness, a creative energy that encompasses the Church.

From one end of the Scriptures to the other, the God of the Covenant reveals Himself as a Spouse who wants to give everything and give Himself despite the limitations and faults of sinful humanity, His Spouse. The jealous and humiliated God never tires of chasing the wandering and idolatrous wife until the blessed day of the Lamb's wedding. This is why the hope of God's gift does not disappoint. "The Spirit and the Bride say, 'Come!' He who hears, let him also say, 'Come!' He who is thirsty, let him come closer. Whoever desires it, let him drink the water of life, free of charge."[266]

Yes Father, we thank You for already pouring Your living water on earth into the hearts of the poorest among the poor, thanks to the tireless dedication of all those consecrated souls who make their existence a sacrament of Your free love.

[264] Ibid.
[265] Jn 4:10.
[266] Rev 22:17.

Friends of the Bridegroom

O Father of all grace, from the inaccessible light where You live and where we are introduced by the Spirit, with Jesus and Mary, we ask You to consume us in unity by consecrating us in truth.

Pour out Your Holy Spirit on us and on all flesh, the Spirit of truth, Who regenerates the faith; the Spirit of freedom, Who resurrects hope; the Spirit of love, Who makes the Church holy, credible, attractive, and missionary.

May Your kingdom come! Thy will be done on earth as it is in Heaven. May Your saving will, fulfilled in Your crucified and glorified Son, also be fulfilled in us priests of the New Covenant and in the souls entrusted to our ministry.

"With the Holy Spirit, who makes spiritual," writes Saint Basil the Great, "it is the readmission to Paradise, the return to the condition of son, the audacity to call God Father; one becomes a participant in the grace of Christ, one is called the son of light, one shares eternal glory."[267]

"If, then, you want to live by the Holy Spirit," writes Saint Augustine, "keep charity, love the truth, desire unity, and you will reach eternity.[268]

We carry within us, poor sinners, the wounds of humanity wounded by crimes, wars, and tragedies. We confess the sins of the world in their crudity and misery with Jesus crucified, convinced that it is grace and truth that set us free. We confess sins in the Church, especially those that are reasons for scandal and alienation of the faithful and unbelievers.

Above all, we confess, Lord, Your Love and Mercy, which radiate from Your Eucharistic heart and from the absolution of sins that we give to the faithful.

[267] Saint Basil the Great, *De Spiritu sancto*, XV, 36.
[268] Saint Augustine, *Sermon 267 for the Day of Pentecost*, 1, *The Holy Spirit Living in the Church*, 4, 4.

The Holy Father has abundantly reminded us of this throughout this Year for Priests:

> Dear priests, what an extraordinary ministry the Lord has entrusted to us! Just as in the Eucharistic celebration, he places himself in the hands of the priest to continue to be present among his people, so he entrusts himself to the priest in the Sacrament of Reconciliation so that men may experience the kiss with which the father once again welcomes the prodigal son, restoring his filial dignity and restoring him fully heir (cf. Lk 15:11-32).[269]

Saint Jean-Marie Vianney tells us again in his own way: "God knows everything. Even before you confess, he already knows that you will sin again and, however, he forgives you. The Love of our God is so great, he goes so far as to voluntarily forget the future, to forgive us."[270]

There at the altar of sacrifice, in union with Mary, we offer Christ to the Father, and we offer ourselves with Him. Let us be aware, dear friends, that by celebrating the Eucharist, we are not doing a human work, but we are offering God to God. "How is that possible?" one could object. It is possible through faith, because faith gives us God. Faith also gives us to God. We have God in a way, as He has us. The One Whom philosophers refer to as the All-Other and the Unavailable *par excellence* wanted to be born and to live among us, man among men, by virtue of a Wisdom that is scandalous for Jews and madness for pagans.[271] In His divine company, we sometimes

---

[269] Benedict XVI, Address to the participants of the course on the internal forum organized by the Apostolic Penitentiary, March 11, 2010.

[270] A. Monnin, *Le Curé d'Ars: Vie de Jean-Baptiste-Marie Vianney*, vol. I, p. 130.

[271] Cf. 1 Cor 1:23.

resemble carefree and rebellious children who rub shoulders with treasures, ready to squander them as if nothing had happened.

What an abyss the mystery of the priesthood is! What wonders the common priesthood of the baptized and the ministerial priesthood are! These sacramental mysteries finally refer to the mystery of God, one and triune. The sacrificial offering of the redeeming Christ is basically the eternal Eucharist of the Son responding to the Love of the Father in the name of all creation. We are associated with this mystery through the Spirit of our baptism, which makes us participants in the divine nature.[272] The more the Spirit makes the baptized alive with divine sonship and the more He makes the priests radiant with divine paternity, the more the two unite in a common epiclesis radiating the world with the glory of the Spirit. "That all may be one, as you, Father, are in me and I am in you, that they may be in us too, so that the world may believe that you have sent me."[273]

Gathered in the Upper Room, invoking the Holy Spirit with Mary, in fraternal communion, we pray for the unity of the Church. The permanent scandal of the division of Christians; the recurrent tensions between clergy, laity, and religious; the laborious harmonization of charisms; the urgency of a new evangelization: all these realities call for a new Pentecost on the Church and the world—first of all, on bishops and priests so that the Spirit of holiness received at their ordination may produce in them new fruits, in the authentic Spirit of the Second Vatican Council. The decree *Presbyterorum Ordinis* defined priestly holiness on the basis of pastoral charity and the requirements of unity of the presbyterium:

> Pastoral charity therefore requires priests, if they do not want to run for nothing, to work in permanent communion with

[272] 2 Pt 1:4.
[273] Jn 17:21.

the bishops and their other brothers in the priesthood. This will be the way for priests to find in the very unity of the Church's mission the unity of their own lives. Thus, they will unite themselves to their Lord, and through him, to the Father, in the Holy Spirit; thus, they will be filled with consolation and overflowing with joy.[274]

Today, as in the early days of the Church, the challenges of evangelization are accompanied by the ordeal of persecution. Let us remember that the credibility of Christ's disciples is measured by the mutual love that allows them to convince the world.[275] "Much more," Saint Paul said to the Romans, "we put our pride in our own distresses, knowing that distress produces perseverance, perseverance produces proven fidelity, proven fidelity, hope; and hope does not deceive, for God's love has been poured into our hearts through the Holy Spirit who has been given to us."[276]

IV. Trinitarian Thanksgiving

Dear friends, let us give thanks to God for the insignia of the priesthood of the New Covenant. By being associated with the oblation of the sacrificed Lamb, we share in the fullness of faith that opens the mysteries of eternal life. Together with Mary, let us let ourselves be charmed and carried away by the Spirit with the choir of angels in the praise of the glory of God three times holy. "May the Holy Spirit make us an eternal offering to your glory."[277]

"I love you, O infinitely kind God, and I would rather die loving you than live a single moment without loving you." Saint Jean-Marie Vianney, patron saint of all priests, lead us in the following

[274] *PO*, no. 14.
[275] Cf. Jn 13:35; 16:8.
[276] Rom 5:3-5.
[277] Eucharistic Prayer III.

of Jesus on the way of intimacy with the Father in the joy of the Holy Spirit, and keep us in the joy of God's service.

Following the example of Saint Jean-Marie Vianney, let us love God with all our hearts in the unity of the Holy Spirit, and let us also love the Church, which is His dwelling place on earth: "We too, then," writes Saint Augustine, "receive the Holy Spirit if we love the Church, if we are companions in charity, if we rejoice in possessing the name of Catholic and the Catholic faith. Believe it, brothers, to the extent that someone loves the Church, he has the Holy Spirit."[278]

Pope John Paul II summarized in two words his priestly existence in the following of Jesus: *Gift* and *Mystery*. Gift of God, Mystery of communion. His great open arms embracing the whole world remain engraved in our memories. They are for us the icon of Christ, Priest and Shepherd, constantly reminding our minds of the essential: the Upper Room, where the Apostles with Mary hope and welcome the Holy Spirit, in joy and praise, in the name of all humanity.

Amen!

[278] Saint Augustine, *Discourse on the Gospel of John*, 32:7-8.

Chapter 6

Mary, the Priest and the Mission[279]

> When Jesus saw his mother and the disciple there whom he
> loved, he said to his mother, "Woman, behold, your son."
> Then he said to the disciple, "Behold, your mother." And
> from that hour the disciple took her into his home.[280]

What I would like to share with you at the end of this symposium
on the priesthood comes from this passage from the Gospel of John,
very dear to the Catholic tradition. Marian piety and ecclesiology
readily refer to it, especially since Pope Paul VI, at the end of the
third session of the Second Vatican Ecumenical Council, declared
Mary to be Mother of the Church.

We remember the famous debate that divided the conciliar
assembly into two almost equal camps and finally ended with the
decision to set out the doctrine on the Virgin Mary not in a separate
document but within the Constitution on the Church. This was
a very important decision for ecclesiology and Mariology, because
these two disciplines risked developing in parallel to the detriment
of both.

---

[279] Colloquium: Priests in the Mystery of the Church: Filiation and
Fatherhood, Fraternity and Sponsorship, Séminaire français de
Rome, January 6, 2012.
[280] Jn 19:26-27.

Friends of the Bridegroom

Some thought that the title "Mother of the Church," decreed by *motu proprio* by Pope Paul VI, marked a step backward in relation to the thought of the Council. But in fact, far from being a concession to the supporters of a maximalist Mariology, this title expresses a Catholic tradition well founded on Sacred Scripture and the Fathers:

> There is no contradiction, writes Father Ignace de la Potterie, in saying that Mary is at the same time image of the Church and Mother of the Church. As an individual person, she is the mother of Jesus, and she becomes the mother of all of us, the mother of the Church. But her bodily motherhood towards Jesus continues in a spiritual motherhood towards believers and towards the Church.[281]

The same exegete notes that in the West, there is a general tendency to see in the Church an organization composed of men, where, at the leadership level, women do not play a major role:

> Indeed, too much and exclusive emphasis has been placed on its institutional and masculine aspect, so that the "Marian face," the "feminine and maternal face," the mystical aspect of the Church has remained in the background.[282]

This limit of Western ecclesiology is undoubtedly not unrelated to the crisis of identity of priests that strongly marked the postconciliar period and has not yet been really resolved. Signs of this crisis are the abandonment of the priesthood, the decline of priestly vocations, the loss of the sense of mystery, especially in liturgy, and the purely functional vision of ministry, to which

---

[281] Ignace de la Potterie, *Mary in the Mystery of the Covenant* (Paris: Desclée, 1988), pp. 246-247.
[282] Ibid., p. 252.

priestly celibacy would add only an extrinsic dimension, purely disciplinary, increasingly contested.

To remedy this crisis of identity that affects priests and, even more profoundly, consecrated life, it is necessary to hear the authors who highlight the "Marian principle"[283] of ecclesiology, according to Hans Urs von Balthasar, vigorously echoed by Joseph Ratzinger:

> The Church is not a mechanical entity; it is not a mere institution, nor one of the usual sociological realities — it is a person. It is a woman. She is a mother. She is alive. The Marian understanding of the Church is the most decisive antithesis to a purely organizational or bureaucratic conception of the Church. We cannot make the Church; we must be the Church. We are the Church, and the Church is in us only to the extent that faith shapes not only our action, but also our being. It is only by being Marian that we become the Church.[284]

Correlatively and more deeply, should we not also recognize another limit of Western theology with regard to the identity of Christ, Spouse of the Church? Even if this Christological title belongs to Sacred Scripture and Tradition, it has been little used as a basis for the Sacrament of Holy Orders. The rise of feminism and its claim to priestly ordination have forced the Magisterium of the Church to develop recently this dimension of Christology and the Sacrament of Orders to justify theologically the constant refusal of the Catholic tradition in this regard.[285]

[283] Hans Urs von Balthasar, *The Anti-Roman Complex: Essay on Ecclesial Structures* (Paris: Apostolat des Éditions, 1976), pp. 191-235.

[284] Joseph Ratzinger, "The Ecclesiology of the Second Vatican Council," *Communio* (English) 13, no. 3 (1986), p. 252.

[285] Saint John Paul II, Post-Synodal Apostolic Exhortation *Pastores Gregis* on the Bishop, Servant of the Gospel of Jesus Christ for the

Friends of the Bridegroom

Without entering into a discussion of these questions, the following reflections outline a deepening of the relationship between Mary and the priesthood, starting from the spiritual motherhood of the Virgin Mary that we mentioned at the beginning. The foundation will be a theology of the Word in a Marian perspective, which will lead us to the center of the mystery of the Bride-Church (I); from there we will deepen the relationship between the Virgin and the priesthood (II), which leads to Mary's relationship with the priest in the Church's mission (III).

I. Mary, Mother of the Church
A. *Servant of the Word*

Every discourse on Mary, Mother of the Church, must begin with the event of divine revelation understood as an encounter between God and man. The Conciliar Constitution on Divine Revelation states: "The invisible God (cf. Col 1:15; 1 Tim 1:17) speaks to men in his superabundant love as friends (cf. Ex 33:11; Jn 15:14-15); he talks with them (cf. Bar 3:38) to invite them and admit them to share his own life."[286] Mary is the archetype *par excellence* of this encounter that establishes a relationship of Covenant.

The Word of God presupposes in itself, to an unsurpassable degree, the acceptance of faith as a constituent element of the Covenant relationship. Already, the Word of God addressed to Abraham, Moses, David, or the prophets always implied a personal

---

Hope of the World, no. 21: "The Pastor stands before his people as Christ, the Spouse, who gave his life for us and left to all the example of a clear and virginal love, and therefore also fertile and universal."

[286] Second Vatican Council, Dogmatic Constitution on Divine Revelation *Dei Verbum*, no. 2.

162

welcome, followed or accompanied by a reading of events in faith, which constituted the treasure of Holy Scripture.

Mary is in a unique way a creature of the Word. Her whole life and mission are defined as a service of the Word: "I am the handmaid of the Lord; may it be done to me according to your word."[287] A theology of the Word in Marian perspective, therefore, begins with the fiat of the Annunciation and ends with the same fiat heroically supported at the Cross. These two key moments symbolically include the whole mystery of the Incarnation of the Word from which Mary's life is inseparable.

Mary's fiat expresses a decision of faith and a permanent attitude of welcome that corresponds to the event of the Word's becoming flesh. Mary belongs to this event, which goes from the first moment of the virginal conception to the death and Resurrection of Christ. In all this deployment, she says yes to God, Who says and gives Himself. Mary does so "in the name of all human nature,"[288] writes Saint Thomas Aquinas. Her presence in the Upper Room on the day of Pentecost testifies to her intimate relationship with the Holy Spirit, Who now extends into the Church the Incarnation of the Word fulfilled in her.

"Thus God, who once spoke, never ceases to converse with the Bride of his beloved Son, and the Holy Spirit, through whom the living voice of the Gospel resounds in the Church and, through the Church, in the world, introduces believers into the whole truth and makes the word of Christ dwell in them with all its richness (cf. Col 3:16)."[289] The conciliar Constitution *Dei Verbum* thus ratifies a theology of the Word in Marian perspective as the foundation of the nuptial ecclesiology we need today.

---

[287] Lk 1:38.
[288] Saint Thomas Aquinas, *Summa Theologica*, IIIa, q. 30, a. 1, ad 4.
[289] *Dei Verbum*, no. 8.

Friends of the Bridegroom

B. *Mater Dolorosa*

The acceptance of the Word in Mary is, in fact, inseparable from the Breath of the Father, Who speaks it in her, in order to realize through her the mystery of the Covenant. For, to be Mother of God, Mary had to be married by God. She was therefore set apart and protected from any fault from the moment of conception, in order to be only yes to grace, yes to divine motherhood, and yes also to spiritual motherhood in relation to the Church, represented by John, the beloved disciple, at the foot of the Cross.

The dying Christ addresses His Mother by calling her "Woman," an appellation that evokes the first woman of Genesis, Eve, the mother of all the living, suggesting that a new dimension of her motherhood was taking shape precisely at this decisive moment in the history of salvation. At the moment of death, Jesus certainly entrusts His Mother to the beloved disciple to take care of her. But the scene means infinitely more than that. Jesus first defines Mary's new motherhood. Let us note that He first addresses her to entrust her with this sinful son in exchange for Himself. Saint Bernard understood better than anyone else the mysterious significance of this word:

> Wasn't it more than a sword to you, did it not pierce your soul and reach to the division of soul and spirit, this word: "Woman, behold your son"? Oh, what an exchange! John is given to you in the place of Jesus, the servant in the place of the Lord, the disciple in the place of the Master, the son of Zebedee in the place of the Son of God, a simple man in the place of the true God. How could listening to this word not pierce your affectionate soul, when the mere memory of this word already breaks our hearts, which are made of rock and iron?[290]

---

[290] Saint Bernard, "Homily for the Sunday after the Assumption", in *Liturgie des Heures*, vol. 4 (Paris: éd. du Cerf, 1980), pp. 997-998.

At this precise moment, as at the moment of the Annunciation, God says what will be: here is your son, which means, I must leave, and you must consent to it, even without understanding. From now on, this one is entrusted to your maternity so that you can shape in him the priesthood you experienced with me. What I was for you and with you, throughout my life to this day, must be continued in the ministers I establish to accomplish the mystery of the Covenant for centuries to come.

Von Balthasar sees in this scene the foundation of the Church's participation in the sacrifice of Calvary, which is the same as the Sacrifice of the Mass: "She attends the self-giving of the Son, unable to intervene; but she is far from being passive; a superhuman action is asked of her: to consent to the sacrifice of this man who is the Son of God, but also her own son."[291]

Mary does not say a new fiat; she remains silent in her pain, because her consent to this unspeakable sacrifice was already included in the grace of the initial yes to the mystery of the Incarnation. She is therefore in all truth the new Eve, the Mater Dolorosa, in whom and through whom the New Adam generates the new humanity. At the foot of the Cross, according to the expression of Saint John Paul II, "maternal cooperation to the whole mission of the Savior is realized through the actions and sufferings of Mary."[292]

C. (Wife) Bride of the Lamb

This mystery of the Covenant, a nuptial mystery if ever there was one, is accomplished in the most complete abandonment, in the

---

[291] H. Urs von Balthasar and Adrienne von Speyr, *Au cœur du mystère redempteur* (Sentiers de lumière, C.L.D., 1980), p. 52.
[292] Saint John Paul II, Encyclical Letter *Redemptoris Mater* on the Blessed Virgin Mary in the Life of the Church in Progress, no. 39.

nakedness of pure love that escapes all human measure. Jesus is stripped of His clothes and nailed to the Cross; the Apostles have fled; the crowd mocks and insults Him; He feels the darkness invading Him: "My God, my God, why have you abandoned me?" Jesus took upon Himself the sin of all; He is the scapegoat for all our hatred and betrayals; He offered Himself to the Father for this, to reveal the love of the Father in this; He the Lamb of God, Who takes away the sin of the world.

At the bottom of this abyss of abandonment, however, He remembers the spotless, wrinkle-free lamb, the one that has been preserved from any fault since her conception, precisely to become one with Him in this mystery of passion and compassion. Being perfectly pure, Mary can be perfectly united with Him, but in a dimension of communion that transcends the bonds of blood.

That is why He now addresses her as He addressed her in Cana: "Woman," meaning a certain distance in the order of the flesh, which allows them to reach together a deeper union in the Spirit. "As the Father abandons his Son, the Son separates from his Mother," writes von Balthasar. "This form of union was necessary so that Mary—who from now on would form the center of the Church—would know from experience the mystery of the Redemption and could transmit it to her new children."[293] This form of painful union is "a purification without personal fault, which must then be a purification so that God can dispose of her as He wishes."[294]

The following words of the Gospel explicitly indicates the scope of Jesus' word by this other word: "All is finished." It sheds light on what has just been said as a decisive fact, an ultimate, eschatological gift. This is further confirmed by the words "I thirst," which

[293] Ibid.
[294] A. von Speyr, *Mary in the Redemption* (San Francisco: Ignatius Press, 2003), p. 80.

summarize all the thirsts of humanity and of God, to Whom vinegar is offered, a symbol of our sinful offerings.

Finally, the story describes the final moment when the dying Jesus bows His head and hands over the Spirit. The death of the Lord is like the death of a sovereign who lays down his crown freely with his last breath. This last breath is the prelude to the gift of the Spirit, according to Johannine exegesis; it already signifies the victory of Love and therefore the success of the Covenant. For the gift of the Holy Spirit confirms the mission of the Messiah-Anointed One, Who, through His Resurrection from the dead, inaugurates the outpouring of the Spirit on all flesh, as announced by the prophets.

Mary welcomes the Gift of the Spirit as she did the Incarnation of the Word: in perfect openness and availability, both in the Upper Room and at the death of her Son. The Holy Spirit will now be her personal link to Christ and the Church: a nuptial bond with the sacrificed Lamb, Spouse of the Church, and a maternal bond to the Church Bride of which she is the inchoate subjectivity and center.[295]

The Spirit of Christ will thus be, inseparably, the Spirit of Mary, the Spirit of the Covenant. This Spirit will now penetrate hearts, bringing peace, reconciliation, divine filiation and ecclesial fraternity enriched by various forms of nuptiality. Among these forms, there is, first of all, that of the spouses in the Sacrament of Marriage; also that of the ordained ministers, sacraments of Christ the Bridegroom; and finally that of consecrated persons whose virginity for the Kingdom incarnates the nuptial love of the Spouse-Church. There is obviously an analogy between these forms of nuptiality, but their common foundation is a charism of the Holy Spirit that

---

[295] H. Urs von Balthasar *Who Is the Church?*, in *Sponsa Verbi*, Morcelliana, pp. 139-187; *The Divine Drama, II: The Persons of Drama, 2. The Persons in Christ*, pp. 271-288.

establishes new spiritual relationships in humanity, in the image of the Holy Family of Nazareth and intra-Trinitarian relationships.

II. Mary and the Priesthood

Having mentioned the spiritual maternity of Mary, which envelops the whole Church, we do not forget that this maternity concerns especially ordained ministers. During this colloquium, the apostolic dimension of the priesthood was discussed, as well as its filial, paternal, and even nuptial dimensions. These dimensions evoke by themselves the Trinitarian foundation of the whole sacramentality of the Church. The mystery of the Church ultimately refers to the Trinitarian mystery of which She is the sacrament. For the seven sacraments are aimed at one thing only: to introduce each person and the ecclesial community into Trinitarian communion. The priesthood of Christ, doubly participated in by the royal priesthood of the baptized and the ministerial priesthood of priests, has meaning only according to the Trinitarian Life to which it gives access.

The figure of Mary, Mother of the Church, at the heart of this vision of the Church, *Sacramentum Trinitatis*, invites us to deepen the relationship between the royal priesthood of the baptized and the particular priesthood of ordained ministers. Mary, being Mother of the Church by her immaculate faith, is associated by the Father with the sacrifice of the Son, which enables her to participate in the outpouring of the Holy Spirit on all flesh. The Holy Spirit has been close and familiar to her since the Annunciation, guiding her unceasingly towards participation in the Paschal Mystery of her Son. Having elevated her to the dignity of the Lamb's Bride, the Spirit at the same time gave her the mission of giving birth to the new humanity with Christ, the New Adam. In doing so, she acquires a prominent and even unique place in the economy of grace, which tradition refers to as the Mediatrix (mediator) of all grace.

The Second Vatican Council took care to affirm that Mary's mediation "does not offend or diminish in any way [the] unique mediation of Christ: on the contrary, [it] manifests its virtue."[296] For the absolutely singular mediation of the Divine Redeemer is not intended to annul all others but, on the contrary, to found them, to restore them, to make all believers capable of being instruments of grace. The mystery of Mary Mediatrix is thus the perfect confirmation of the overabundance of Christ's grace.

The mystery of the priesthood in the Church is nothing more than the expression of this mediation of grace, which is first and foremost the work of all the baptized, but also and in a particular way the work of ordained ministers. The priesthood of the baptized is filial in nature, because it results from participation in the divine Sonship of Jesus. It belongs to all as disciples, and it includes an authentic mediation of grace, which consists in the exercise of the theological virtues in all the worship and apostolic activities that follow. Mary exercises this priesthood in fullness, to the point that her maternal mediation envelops and even founds the ministerial priesthood.

The priesthood of priests and bishops is of a ministerial nature. It deploys a specific dimension of Christ's mediation, that of His representation of the Father. For the Son was incarnated to communicate divine life to humanity. He communicates His filial life through Baptism and the life of the Father through the ministerial priesthood. The Holy Spirit crowns these two essentially distinct forms of priesthood, multiplying the charisms that enrich both forms. The many institutes of consecrated life, old and new, bear witness to the inexhaustible fruitfulness of the royal and ministerial priesthood in the Church.

Thus, Mary fully exercises the royal priesthood. She is, in and through Christ, the source and summit of it. Mary is therefore not

[296]LG, no. 60.

only the unsurpassable model of the fertile faith of the disciples; she is the mother of the hierarchical priesthood. For there would be no ministerial representation of Christ, Head and Spouse, in the Church, if the Bride-Church were not first constituted by the personal and enveloping presence of Mary. At all stages of the Incarnation of the Word and the life of the Church, there is Mary's faith, which guarantees the Church's participation in the life and sacrifice of the one Mediator.

The admirable exchange at the foot of the Cross illustrates the paradox of Mary's spiritual motherhood. Indeed, her fullness of grace depends entirely on the Cross, and yet Mary participates in *actu primo redemptionis* in the sacrifice of the sacrificed Lamb. "For the solidarity that Christ wants to establish between himself and his Church is not satisfied with a faith granted *post factum*, but requires simultaneous, instantaneous consent, so that his sacrifice is truly total: inseparably that of the head and the members."[297] Only in this way can we establish that the one sacrifice of Christ, on the Cross and at Mass, is at the same time the sacrifice of the Church — an infinitely fruitful sacrifice of the Head and limbs, the Bridegroom and the Bride.

Mary's spiritual motherhood therefore nourishes the filial life of God's children as well as the paternal charism of bishops and priests. All grace and mission in the Church, and, above all, that of hierarchical ministry, are indebted to Mary and cannot be exercised in a lasting, fruitful way without a vital relationship with the mother of the priesthood. One can then guess that the priest's devotion to the Virgin Mary is not a sentimental and superfluous growth of his spirituality, but rather the source and vital sap that ensure his permanent regeneration.

[297] H. Urs von Balthasar, op. cit., p. 53.

III. Mary and the priest

"From that hour on, the disciple took her into his home."[298] This is the translation of the end of verse 27 proposed by Father de la Potterie, on the basis of his in-depth studies on the Gospel of John. The Greek expression is more vague, he says, but this translation seems to him to be the most faithful to "the meaning that John probably gave it."[299] The immediate context is indeed the last will of Jesus, His testament in a way: He wants His own intimacy with His Mother to be prolonged in that of His beloved disciple. This determination of the Lord means that the life and apostolic ministry of the disciple will be inhabited, supported, and enriched by the presence and fullness of His Mother's graces. Each priest enjoys this privilege by virtue of his friendship with the Master. "I no longer call you slaves, because a slave does not know what his master is doing. I have called you friends, because I have told you everything I have heard from my Father."[300]

This intimacy of the priest with the Mother of the Lord must color his whole life and activities, thus bringing a special grace of mercy and fruitfulness to his ministry. Just think of the Curé d'Ars and John Paul II to be convinced of this. Their universally recognized radiance would be inexplicable without this reference to Mary's motherhood, so present and fertile in their intimate lives. "Is it foolhardy to assume," writes André Feuillet, "that it was under the secret influence of Mary that John was able to write the last word of Christian revelation: God is Love?"[301]

---

[298] Jn 19:27.

[299] I. de la Potterie, *The Passion of Jesus according to the Gospel of John: Text and Spirit*, Lire la Bible (Paris, éd. du Cerf, 1986), p. 163.

[300] Jn 15:15.

[301] André Feuillet, *Jésus et sa mère, d'après les récits lucaniens de l'enfance et d'après Saint Jean: Le rôle de la Vierge Marie dans l'histoire du salut et la place de la femme dans l'Église* (Paris: J. Gabalda, 1974), p. 219.

Friends of the Bridegroom

This living intimacy of the priest with Mary is the concrete and effective way of recognizing that the Church is not first and foremost an institution or an organization, but rather a Person, Who has a personal face and attitudes, of which Mary, as Mother and Spouse, is the symbol *par excellence*. Seeing the Church from Mary prevents us from degrading it to the rank of a sociological reality without interiority or unity. On the other hand, a priest nourished by Marian ecclesiology has his ministry enhanced, as well as his lifestyle and fervor. His relationship with his peers and the community will be more humane and personalized, to the great benefit of the faithful, who will feel treated with respect and concern.

On the other hand, where the disciple's intimate relationship with the Mother of God is lacking, his commitment to celibacy becomes less joyful and more laborious; the risk of sterile activism increases; his prayer may lack breath, as well as enthusiasm for his vocation, which is not without consequences for the emergence of new vocations.

When a priest prays and offers the Eucharist in union with her; when he announces the Word received from her in faith; and when he consents to the sacrifice of certain affections and preferences, supported intimately by her intercession, the priest extends the priesthood of Christ in a way that gives glory to God and honors the Church.[302] His availability, serenity, and apostolic zeal are strengthened and protected from bitterness during the inevitable failures of pastoral life.

---

[302] *PDV*, no. 29: "The will of the Church finds its final motivation in the link of celibacy with Sacred Ordination, which configures the priest to Jesus Christ, Head and Spouse of the Church. The Church, as Spouse of Jesus Christ, wants to be loved by the priest in the total and exclusive way in which Jesus Christ, Head and Spouse, loved her. Priestly celibacy, then, is a gift of self in and with Christ to his Church, and it expresses the service rendered by the priest to the Church in and with the Lord."

The reasons for encouraging the priest's Marian devotion are therefore multiple, and we instinctively guess their importance. The essential thing, however, is to recognize their theological foundation: the Lord's express willingness to grant His Mother a vital role in the mystery of redemption and in the mission of each priest. Jesus wanted His Mother to be in a special way the model and Mother of priests. "Indeed," writes André Feuillet, "every priest worthy of the name is not content to represent Christ the Priest sacramentally. He understands that he is bound, more than others, to realize the ideal of the royal priesthood by entering into the sacrificial and victimal dispositions of the One he represents. Better than anyone else, Mary made these provisions her own."[303]

Mary's spiritual motherhood embraces all the dimensions of grace in the Church and in humanity, and she knows better than anyone else the place and importance of the priesthood of priests in this economy: "Now," adds the great exegete of Saint John, "she [Mary] contemplates in priests the extensions and images of Christ the Priest, her Son, and she has only one desire, which is to make these images as close as possible to Christ. She therefore leads the priests in her wake as a Mother leads her children after her."[304] She wants them to be holy as her Son and she obtains for them all the graces necessary to their condition, especially if they ask her, by virtue of their intimacy with her, which guarantees special access to the Lord.

Conclusion

What can we conclude at the end of this meditation on Mary and the priesthood?

[303] André Feuillet, op. cit.
[304] Ibid., p. 247.

Friends of the Bridegroom

The Christian West is going through an unprecedented identity crisis, which threatens not only the future of its institutions, but above all the transmission of the faith to future generations, in the absence of priests available for evangelization. At the heart of this crisis, the question of women is essential both from the point of view of cultural and ideological phenomena and from the point of view of ecclesiology, in order to restore the value of their fundamental role as mothers and wives.

The Church's efforts to engage priests in the new evangelization will succeed, in my humble opinion, if their love of Christ and the Church is regenerated at the source of the faith of the Star-Crowned Woman, whose motherhood embraces the whole mystery of the priesthood in the Church. Since the crisis of identity of priests is, above all, a crisis of faith and love, would not its solution depend on the disciple's renewed response to the Lord's will: "Behold your mother"?

Part 3

For a Priestly Spirituality in the School of Saints

I no longer call you slaves, because a slave does not know what his master is doing. I have called you friends, because I have told you everything I have heard from my Father.

—John 15:15

Chapter 7

Exemplary Figures of Priests[305]

I make you a watchman.[306]

Rather, God chose the foolish of the world to shame the wise, and God chose the weak of the world to shame the strong.[307]

Dear friends,

AUGUST 13, 1815–AUGUST 13, 2015. Two hundred years since that August 13, 1815, when Deacon Jean-Marie Vianney received his priestly ordination from Bishop Simon of Grenoble. This is a memorable date for the local Church and for the universal Church, because this country priest belongs to the cohort of first-rate saints who have left an unquenchable trail of light in history. Raised to the altar in 1925, almost at the same time as Saint Thérèse of the Child Jesus, he shared with her the message of merciful love that paved the way for the renewal of evangelization in our time. Since the Second Vatican Ecumenical Council, the Popes have

[305] Homily in Ars, August 4, 2015. See Ezek 3:16-21; 1 Cor 1:26-29; Mt 9:26-29.
[306] Ezek 3:17.
[307] 1 Cor 1:27.

developed this theme in crescendo until Pope Francis proclaimed an extraordinary Jubilee of Mercy.

On August 13, 1815, Jean-Marie Vianney, twenty-nine years and three months old, honorably passed his theological exams, despite the almost insurmountable obstacle of Latin. Many personal, family, and national trials have immersed his character, purified his soul, and confirmed his vocation. He has finally succeeded in fulfilling his dream of ascending to the altar of God to offer the Holy Sacrifice. His dimissory letters authorize ordination without, however, the Ordinary's granting him the faculties to hear confessions. Jean-Marie is not offended by this; he is too happy that God's mercy has looked upon him with compassion, despite his unworthiness and limitations: "God chose the weak of the world," writes Saint Paul to the Corinthians, "to shame the strong, and God chose the lowly and despised of the world, those who count for nothing, to reduce to nothing those who are something."[308]

In post-revolutionary France, subject to a "dictatorship of rationalism,"[309] God chose this poor and poorly educated peasant to confuse those who claim to be something without God. Pope Francis's motto, *Miserando atque eligendo*, inspired by a commentary by Saint Bede the Venerable on Matthew's vocation, fits quite well with the vocation of the young Jean-Marie Vianney. This one has no moral defect, but he is chosen in spite of his limitations precisely to bring out the merciful glory of God in his ministry as a country priest. "He may not be very well educated," said Bishop Devie, to defend him, "but he is enlightened."

While cardinals and bishops of the time were busy playing the political game according to the legitimate or imposed authority of the moment, Jean-Marie Vianney was ordained almost in secret and

[308] 1 Cor 1:27-28.
[309] Cf. Benedict XVI.

sent a little later to the lost sheep of the Lyon country, in this obscure and little-esteemed village on the ecclesiastical map of the region. *Miserando atque eligendo*: Jesus saw Matthew, the publican, sitting at his tax collector's table; He looked at him with mercy (*miserando*) and chose (*eligendo*) this sinner, whom His grace would transform into an Apostle. In a similar way, Jesus saw this poor peasant, despised by the world but precious in the eyes of God, and transformed him by His grace into an effective confessor of a multitude of sinners.

When Jesus saw the crowds, He was seized with compassion for them, because they were helpless and worn out, like sheep without a shepherd. "Thus," John Paul II preached, "Christ stopped here in Ars at the time when Jean-Marie Vianney was parish priest there. Yes, he stopped. He saw the 'crowds' of the men and women of the last century, who were 'tired and worn out' like sheep without a shepherd (Mt 9:36)."[310]

Christ stopped at Jean-Marie Vianney's parish to grant him the much desired conversion of his parish. He stopped to expel unclean spirits, to drive out ignorance, to visit the poor, and to heal all disease and infirmity. He stopped to suffer with the holy Curé, to inspire his preaching, to console the afflicted, and to drive out the darkness of sin.

Between the daily offering of Christ's Sacrifice and the immolation of his own body, which had been severely reduced to servitude, there was no frontier; the Love of the Heart of Jesus united the mystery of the priesthood and the ministry of the holy priest in a single, infallibly fulfilled offering. Hence the prodigies of mercy that pacified the thousands of pilgrims who flocked to his confessional. The holy priest listened attentively; sometimes he completed the partial confessions; sometimes he cried for insufficient contrition; often he gave the usual penance and reserved the right to complete

[310]Saint John Paul II, homily in Ars, October 6, 1986.

it personally; always he scrupulously served the divine mercy, even when he imposed a delay on absolution.

For if the Curé d'Ars was the very icon of the Good Shepherd; he never separated love and truth. He cared too much about the salvation of souls to absolve them mechanically and indiscriminately. He wanted full mercy and full conversion, even if it meant shaking the penitent with his word and his attitude, just as he watched over the good morals of his parishioners. He fulfilled the word of the prophet Ezekiel:

> Son of man, I have appointed you a sentinel for the house of Israel. When you hear a word from my mouth, you shall warn them for me. If I say to the wicked, You shall surely die—and you do not warn them or speak out to dissuade the wicked from their evil conduct in order to save their lives—then they shall die for their sin, but I will hold you responsible for their blood.[311]

In the first decade of his pastorate, he was certainly found to be a pest. He was close to his flock and was interested in their problems, but he did not tolerate blasphemy, contempt for Sundays, and the cultivation of vices in cabarets. It was not uncommon for him to use the threat of Hell to force the recalcitrant. Moreover, it was not his long sermons, his green corrections, and his excessive penances that brought about the conversion of the faithful, but rather the Love of the Heart of Jesus, which burned in his own heart and shone in his eyes and on his face as a child of God and father of the poor. Whoever saw him praying in the presence of the Blessed Sacrament was struck by his attitude, his gestures, and his tears. "He's here," he sighed. "I gaze at him, and he gazes at me," he replied, like the peasant he had once asked about his prayer.

[311] Ezek 3:17-18.

Saint Jean-Marie Vianney knew how to be the watchman who admonished sinners and ruled his community in the name of God, but he conquered them through his prayer, his humility, his patience, his tender devotion to the Virgin Mary. "Building the Church! This is what the Curé d'Ars did in this village."[312] In fact, his forty-one years of pastoral service as a country priest have inspired priests, bishops, and popes, as well as writers and poets, who have paid him sincere and lasting tributes. In short, he was recognized as the Love of the Heart of Jesus, the passage of Christ in his pastoral charity and in his Eucharistic life to the Trinitarian and Marian harmonics.

His ordination was celebrated by a neighboring bishop, alone, almost in secret, without friends or family, but his funeral was an apotheosis, an endless homage, a unanimous chorus of praise and gratitude from the crowds of beneficiaries of his apostolate. What a turnaround, revealing God's merciful kindness towards His people, in this sweet France that was once called the eldest daughter of the Church! On this two hundredth anniversary of the priestly ordination of the Curé d'Ars, what can we do to celebrate the event with dignity, if not ask the Master of the harvest to send workers like Him to His harvest? "Yes, Lord, You, the Good Shepherd Who watches over Your flock, send holy workers of all kinds for the mission of the Church; but in honor of Saint Jean-Marie Vianney, send especially holy priests for the pastoral care of parishes."

May these priests with a heart of fire evangelize with the contagious joy of their witness. May they certainly care about their own sanctification, but may their passion be, above all, the sanctification of God's people, especially this immense crowd of the poor, disoriented and scattered by so many discordant messages. At the time of the Great Jubilee of Mercy, let us beg God to grant us,

---

[312] Saint John Paul II, homily in Ars, October 6, 1986.

through the intercession of the Holy Father, a new outpouring of the Spirit of holiness on priests, so that the missionary conversion of the Church promoted by Francis may finally take the form of a renewed pastoral care of mercy.

May the ever-present testimony of the Curé d'Ars confirm our certainties of faith, strengthen our moral convictions, and above all, awaken our confidence in the grace of God, Who freely chooses what is weak and modest to confuse the wise and the proud.

Oh! Spirit of Jesus Christ, Who one day took possession of this humble peasant from the Lyon country, renew in us the joy of our first love, drive the darkness out of our hearts, and give us to follow more firmly the Good Shepherd in the humble service of the people entrusted to our care. Blessed and thanked be the Lord for the graces you grant us on this feast day when we feel the presence of the Virgin Mary, the Angels and the saints who inspired the holy pastor.

Saint Jean-Marie Vianney, patron saint of priests all over the world, pray for us!

Amen!

* * *

The Holy Priest of Ars: two hundredth anniversary of priestly ordination[313]

On Wednesday, August 9, 1815, Father Vianney presented himself at the offices of the Archbishopric of Lyon, where the vicar-general, Monsignor Courbon, delivered his testimonial letters to him. These letters attested that the bishop of Grenoble could ordain him for the diocese of Lyon, under the clause, however, that the new priest would only later, at the discretion of his Ordinary, have the power to absolve sins.

[313]Conference in Ars, August 3, 2015.

Under the August sun, Father Vianney made the trip on foot, alone, carrying a small package with some provisions and an alb for his first Mass. A hundred kilometers separate Lyon from Grenoble. The aspirant to the priesthood, who felt as light as air, cheerfully crossed this long distance, but not without danger, because France was once again invaded and occupied, this time by the Austrians.

He was received at the major seminary of Grenoble, where he was welcomed the next day by Bishop Simon, a deeply pious prelate, who had ordained him deacon on June 23. For a moment, the bishop contemplated this deacon with an ascetic face, whom neither a relative nor a friend accompanied. To the aspirant's apology for disturbing him, he replied with a grave smile: "It is not too much trouble to ordain a good priest."[314]

The holy priest did not make many confidences on that morning of August 13, 1815, when he received the sublime dignity of the Catholic priesthood. He was twenty-nine years and three months old, and finally, after so many uncertainties, failures, and tears, his dream of being a priest came true. Finally, the sanctuary opened before him where he could celebrate Holy Mass: "Oh, how great is the priest!" he sometimes cried out during catechism. "The priest will only understand himself well in Heaven.... If we understood him on earth, we would die, not of fear but of love!"[315]

It was only several months after his ordination that he was to receive the necessary powers to hear confessions. He was then vicar of Ecully, where Monsignor Balley, the pastor, who had been the patient and farsighted formator of this peasant, was the first penitent to fall to his knees to receive the grace of absolution. Countless

---

[314] Msgr. Francis Trochu, *Le Curé d'Ars: Saint Jean-Marie-Baptiste Vianney* (Montsûrs: Résiac, 2010), p. 122.

[315] A. Monnin, *Spirit of the Priest d'Ars*, p. 113, quoted in Msgr. Trochu, *Le Curé d'Ars*, p. 123.

repentant souls would follow who enjoyed the same grace, forming a procession that grew each year until reaching the number of
eighty thousand pilgrims to Ars in 1858. Benedict XVI recalled
this multitude on August 5, 2009, on the occasion of the Year for
Priests, decreed in honor of the 150th anniversary of the death of
the holy Curé d'Ars: "What a great feast there must have been in
Paradise for the arrival of such a zealous pastor! What welcome must
have been given to him by the multitude of sons reconciled with
the Father, thanks to his work as parish priest and confessor!"[316]

In his Letter of Proclamation for a Year for Priests, Benedict
XVI echoed the profound and moving expression of the Curé d'Ars,
"The priesthood is the Love of the Heart of Jesus." "This touching expression allows us, above all, to evoke with tenderness and
gratitude the immense gift that priests are, not only for the Church,
but also for humanity itself."[317] Indeed, their words, their actions,
their lifestyle, their whole being bear the witness of Christ at the
heart of the Church and of humanity. "But," the Pope adds, "the
expression used by the Holy Priest also evokes the pierced Heart
of Christ and the crown of thorns that surrounds him."[318] This
means the sacrificial dimension of priestly life: compassion for so
many painful situations, the test of fidelity and also the suffering
of the infidelity of a few, widely denounced, as well as the growing
misunderstanding they encounter, sometimes accompanied by
persecutions that can lead to martyrdom.

These few allusions to the condition of priests in our time are
not unrelated to the circumstances experienced by Jean-Marie Vianney. Born during the revolution into a deeply Christian peasant

[316] Benedict XVI, General Audience, Wednesday, August 5, 2009.
[317] Benedict XVI, *Letter for the Proclamation of a Year for Priests on the Occasion of the 150th Anniversary of the "Dies Natalis" of the Holy Curé d'Ars*, 2009.
[318] Ibid.

family, he grew up in a home where unity and charity towards the poor reigned and where faith was lived at the risk of deadly reprisals, particularly because of the hospitality given to refractory priests being pursued by the police. The child made his First Communion at the age of nine in an isolated room in a private house, with all windows closed, to avoid attracting the attention of the revolutionary authorities.

At that time, most parishes were without priests or were served by constitutionalist priests from whom the faithful fled. After the revolutionary storm and the Napoleonic adventure, ecclesial life was able to resume with the means at hand, on the ruins left by the rationalist fury. Everything had to be rebuilt—faith, mores, communities, brotherhoods, works of mercy. If there was a time of new evangelization in the history of France, it was the period of the four decades during which Jean-Marie Vianney was parish priest of Ars.

On the occasion of this anniversary, I think it is appropriate to mention the priestly figure of the holy priest, bearing in mind Pope Francis's call for a pastoral conversion:

> I hope that all the communities will make sure to implement the necessary means to advance on the path of a pastoral and missionary conversion, which cannot leave things as they are. It is not a "simple administration" that we need. Let us constitute ourselves in all regions of the world into a "permanent state of mission."[319]

How can the Curé d'Ars help us to evangelize our time, so different from his by so many factors, such as urban culture, communications, the Internet, and so forth? What were his method,

---

[319] EG, no. 25, with reference to the Fifth General Conference of the Latin American and Caribbean Bishops, *Aparecida Document*, June 29, 2007, nos. 201, 551.

his means, and his secret for the small village of Ars to become a model missionary community for post-revolutionary France? Why not also draw on the heritage of Ars nowadays to evangelize our secularized world? Is not this exemplary pastor a precious resource for carrying out the pastoral conversion desired by the Holy Father as a witness to the good news of mercy?

This good news requires a renewed announcement of mercy, which includes a revival of the sacrament for which Jean-Marie Vianney is renowned. "I insist once again," writes Francis in *Evangelii Gaudium*,

> God never tires of forgiving us; we are the ones who tire of seeking his mercy. Christ, who told us to forgive one another "seventy times seven" (Mt 18:22) has given us his example: he has forgiven us seventy times seven. Time and time again he bears us on his shoulders. No one can strip us of the dignity bestowed upon us by this boundless and unfailing love.[320]

The Curé d'Ars lived this good news and made his poor peasants discover it by being in the midst of his people, according to the beautiful encyclical of Saint John XXIII, "a model of priestly asceticism, a model of piety and especially of Eucharistic piety, a model of pastoral zeal."[321] On the occasion of the two hundredth anniversary of his priestly ordination, I would like to complete this perspective by suggesting that the holiness of the Curé d'Ars perhaps lies above all in his creativity and determination to awaken and make the priesthood of the baptized grow. To this end, I will recall some memories and testimonies that reveal Jean-Marie Vianney

[320] *EG*, no. 3.
[321] Saint John XXIII, Encyclical Letter on the occasion of the centenary of the death of Saint John the Baptist Vianney *Sacerdotii Nostri Primordia*, 1959.

as a pastor of souls, educator of the faith, and hero of spiritual warfare in the perspective of the new evangelization.

I. A pastor with a burning heart

Let us begin with the famous formula that summarizes the fervent vision of the holy priest: "The priesthood is the Love of the Heart of Jesus." This magnificent formula describes the essence of the priest's mission and holiness. The Second Vatican Council expressed the same reality by saying that priests who lead the very life of the Good Shepherd "will find in the exercise of pastoral charity the bond of priestly perfection that will bring their life and action back to unity."[322] For the Curé d'Ars, this formula expresses, first of all, his inner life, his burning heart as a pastor, his awareness of being the depository of a mystery of love that is at the source of his prayer life and of his entire apostolate. Hence, a first major feature of his spirituality, too forgotten, was his devotion to the Holy Trinity. The love of Jesus' Heart is the encounter of transfigured humanity with the eternal Life of Trinitarian relationships. Here are some testimonies reported by Bernard Nodet in his book on the thoughts and heart of Jean-Marie Vianney.[323]

In his breviary at the beginning of his service he had an image of the Holy Trinity pasted on, which constantly reminded him of the foundation and the ABCs of the Christian faith. From his teaching, some pearls were retained by witnesses: "Oh, how beautiful, my children! The Father is our Creator, the Son is our Redeemer, and the Holy Spirit is our leader."[324] "We bless with all our heart

---

[322] Second Vatican Council, Decree on the Ministry and Life of Priests *Presbyterorum Ordinis*, no. 14.

[323] Bernard Nodet, *Jean-Marie Vianney: Curé d'Ars* (Le Puy-Paris: ed. Xavier Mappus, 1958).

[324] A. Monnin, *Esprit du Curé d'Ars*, op. cit. p. 77 (hereafter: *Esprit*), in Nodet, *Vianney*, p. 47.

and with the deepest respect the Most Holy and August Trinity."[325] His devotion to the Trinity is not abstract; it is addressed concretely to the divine Persons, Whose love envelops the creatures: "A Christian, the object of the complaisances of the three divine Persons."[326] "When we pray or come to church to pray, we please the Three Persons of the Holy Trinity."[327]

The love of Jesus' Heart refers to this burning home of the love of the three divine Persons that dwells in the heart of every pastor. He moves this one according to the filial Spirit to the Father, from Whom we must "await our reward when we are 'at home' in the paternal house."[328] His vision of the Father is tender and merciful despite the hints of Jansenism that Vianney had to fight: "There are some who give the Eternal Father a hard heart. Oh! How wrong they are! The Eternal Father, in order to disarm his righteousness, gave his Son an excessively good heart: one does not give what one does not have."[329]

This excessively good Heart of Jesus reveals, in fact, the heart of the Father, Who draws us through Him: "O Jesus, to know you is to love you! ... If we knew how much Our Lord loves us, we would die of pleasure! I don't think there are hearts hard enough not to love when they see themselves so loved.... Charity is so beautiful! It is a flow from the Heart of Jesus, who is all love."[330] The holy priest was inexhaustible on this subject, and he was saddened that few souls responded to this love. Catherine Lassagne reports that "by speaking

---

[325] Azun de Bernétas, *Biography*, in Nodet, *Vianney*, p. 47.

[326] *Esprit*, p. 164, in Nodet, *Vianney*, p. 47.

[327] Catherine Lassagne, *Petit Mémoire sur Monsieur Vianney*, p. 33, in Nodet, *Vianney*, p. 48.

[328] *Esprit*, op. cit., p. 22, Nodet, *Vianney*, p. 48.

[329] *Esprit*, op. cit., p. 25; Monnin, *Le Curé d'Ars*, p. 429, in Nodet, *Vianney*, p. 48.

[330] Nodet, *Vianney*, p. 50.

of this immense love of the so good Heart of Our Lord, his heart was tightening and he could no longer speak, for he was crying."[331]

Let us not fear that the Holy Spirit will be left behind by the Holy Father. On the contrary, he never ceases to use eloquent metaphors to describe his action:

> The Holy Spirit is the conductor of the soul; without Him, it can do nothing. The soul possessed by Him is like a grape from which comes out a delicious liqueur when pressed. Without the Holy Spirit the soul is like a stone from which nothing can be drawn.[332]

> So it's a question of who leads us. If it is not the Holy Spirit, no matter how we do it, there is no substance or flavor in everything we do. If it is the Holy Spirit, there is a soft sweetness.... It's to die for pleasure![333]

> You can feel in these expressions a man who speaks from experience.

> It is the Holy Spirit who sets the fire and the good works commence.[334]

> It should be said every morning: "My God, send me your Spirit who makes me know what I am and what you are."[335]

One of the most common topics of his speeches was the action of the Holy Spirit on souls. He talked about it to everyone, so much

[331] Lassagne, *Petit Mémoire*, pp. 36-39, in Nodet, *Vianney*, p. 54.
[332] Joseph Toccanier, in *Procès de l'Ordinaire*, p. 123; Monnin, *Le Curé d'Ars*, p. 455; *Esprit*, p. 455; Frère Athanase in *Procès*, p. 670, in Nodet, *Vianney*, p. 55.
[333] *Procès*, p. 1097; *Esprit*, p. 80; Monnin, *Le Curé d'Ars*, p. 456, in Nodet, *Vianney*, pp. 55-56.
[334] *Esprit*, p. 84, in Nodet, *Vianney*, p. 57.
[335] *Esprit*, p. 85; Monnin, *Le Curé d'Ars*, p. 459, in Nodet, *Vianney*, p. 57.

so that Father Lacordaire wrote to him one day: "You have taught me to know the Holy Spirit."[336]

In this Trinitarian light of the love of the three divine Persons, it is not surprising that the Curé d'Ars preached ardently the love of God, more than any other truth: "The only happiness we have on earth is to love God and to know that God loves us."[337] "God loves us more than the best of fathers, more than the most tender mother. All we have to do is submit and surrender to his will, with the heart of a child."[338] What better way to awaken the priesthood of the baptized than through this confession of love?

From his first appointment, the new priest had heard Monsignor Courbon's warning: "There is little love of God in that parish; you will be the one to put it there."[339] Towards the end of his life, his instructions and catechisms almost always touched on the love of God, says Catherine Lassagne: "Sometimes he started another subject and always came back to love, especially the charity and goodness of the Sacred Heart of Jesus, his goodness for men."[340] In short, the holy priest carried in his heart a burning flame that sprang unceasingly from the first of the great mysteries of faith, the Holy Trinity, of which he was the icon through his union with the Heart of Jesus.

II. Educator of the faith of a people

As much as the Love of the Heart of Jesus united him to God in prayer, so much did this same love consume him for the conversion

---

[336] Frère Athanase in *Procès*, p. 670, in Nodet, *Vianney*, p. 58.

[337] *Esprit*, p. 304; Pierre Oriol, *Le Prêtre de Village*, p. 61, in Nodet, *Vianney*, p. 59.

[338] Monnin, *Le Curé d'Ars*, p. 311; Frère Athanase in *Procès*, p. 806 in Nodet, *Vianney*, p. 59.

[339] Benedict XVI, Letter of Proclamation for a Year for Priests.

[340] Lassagne, *Petit Mémoire*, p. 53, in Nodet, *Vianney*, p. 74.

of his parish. "My God," he begged, "grant me the conversion of my parish; I agree to suffer whatever you want all the time in my life! ... Yes, for a hundred years the most severe pains, provided they are converted."[341] To obtain this grace, he combined incessant prayer with penance, often excessive in his youth: fasting, hair shirts, sleep deprivation, flogging, and so on. One day he told a young priest in formation the secret of his first conquests: "When I was alone, and I was for eight to nine years, able to make myself comfortable, I sometimes did not eat for whole days.... I then obtained from God everything I wanted, for myself and for others."[342]

This conversion was the result of an abundance of prayer and penance, but it was also the result of an intense and persevering apostolic struggle against the common evils of the time: religious ignorance, Sunday work, cabarets and blasphemy as well as dances. The holy priest was not satisfied with a poor return to religious practice; he aimed for a total and lasting conversion, and he did not let go until the morals of his faithful were in keeping with an authentic Christian life.

To this end, he practiced tirelessly the ministry of catechist—for children first of all, whom he knew how to attract and correct, but also for adults on Sundays. "Thanks to the tireless repetitions of the man of God, the children of Ars became the best educated in the region."[343]

His devouring zeal was exercised, above all, through preaching to the faithful. He carefully prepared his sermons with the resources of the time, which he consulted carefully—copying paragraphs, laboriously developing long book presentations—but then recited

---

[341] Article du Postulateur, Msgr. Boscredon, *Procès apostolique ne pereant*, no. 134, p. 73.
[342] F. Trochu, *Le Curé d'Ars*, p. 160.
[343] Ibid., p. 167.

them with conviction. A loud voice, not very eloquent, sometimes lost in his papers, he had nothing to attract recalcitrant people, especially since he did not miss an opportunity to denounce vices and abuses, especially dance, which was rooted in local mores. "Father," asked a person, "why do you speak so low when you pray and so loud when you preach?" "It is because while I preach," he replied happily, "I speak to deaf people or people who are sleeping, but when I pray, I speak to the good Lord, who is not deaf."[344]

At first, cabarets competed with the church, especially on Sundays, and caused all kinds of evils: blasphemy, drunkenness, infidelity, poverty. The priest succeeded in abolishing them, even at the cost of his own money for the cabaret owner, who was forced to change his profession.

The struggle against the dances was longer and caused him to be quibbled against and slandered, but he led it without quarter until the complete victory, which did not exclude healthy forms of family and popular celebrations. He thus obtained solid and lasting conversions, which gradually transformed the small village into a model parish, where Christian virtues are seriously practiced, and where Sunday was sanctified as the Lord's Day. He added to the extinction of vices the promotion of good works of piety and charity. He founded the Brotherhood of the Holy Rosary and, a little later, La Providence, an original school and a model of popular education. His pedagogy was harsh and tenacious, because he wanted the good of his parishioners, not hesitating to postpone or even refuse absolution when the conversion of penitents was lacking.

During his visit to Ars in 1986, John Paul II recalled:

His parish quickly took on a new face, and he himself did not fail to visit the sick and their families on the spot. He

---

[344]Lassagne, *Petit Mémoire*, first essay, p. 10, in F. Trochu, *Le Curé d'Ars*, pp. 169-170.

was especially concerned about the poor, the orphans of "La Providence," the uneducated children. He brought the girls together. He strengthened fathers and mothers in their educational responsibilities. He brought together brotherhoods. He encouraged the cooperation of the parishioners who, in a way, took charge of the works. He brought in collaborators, whom he trained. He implemented the popular missions. He educated in prayer and missionary assistance."[345]

All this developed in about ten years, punctuated by opposition and denunciations, even to the diocesan authorities, on the part of some priests of the region.

We will never know the graces of conversion that the parish priest obtained through his prayers and especially through the celebration of the Holy Sacrifice.... There was a revolution in our hearts.... The grace was so strong that very few could resist.... Almost everyone worked with all their strength to get out of sin. Human respect was overthrown: people were ashamed of not doing good and not practicing their religion. We could see the serious and thoughtful men; we could hear some of them who had not approached the holy court for a long time saying out loud on the roads: "I want to confess!" All were in holy dispositions. The parish priest said these words to them in an instruction: "My brothers, Ars is no longer Ars! I have confessed and preached in jubilees, in missions. I didn't find anything like this."[346]

This transformation had cost the pastor dearly, but he could now count on a community that supported him, obeyed him, and effectively prevented him from fleeing pastoral responsibility to

[345] Saint John Paul II, Homily in Ars, October 6, 1986.
[346] F. Trochu, *Le Curé d'Ars*, pp. 257-258.

places of penance and atonement, where he would have wanted so much to "mourn his poor life."

In short, the pastoral charity of the good parish priest has not only converted his parish, it has succeeded in associating it and involving it in his own priestly witness, by reviving the grace of Baptism, the fervent exercise of theological and moral virtues and the practice of effective charity for as many people as possible. Hence the influence of this parish of Ars, which became famous because of its profound transformation and which would soon welcome thousands of pilgrims in search of peace with the pastor who had evangelized and educated his people.

Benedict XVI recalls in this context that the Fathers of the Second Vatican Ecumenical Council affirmed "that it is for priests, 'as educators of the faith,' to form 'an authentic Christian community' capable of 'opening the way to all men to Christ' and exercising 'a true motherhood' towards them, indicating or facilitating to those who do not believe 'a path to Christ and his Church' and 'to awaken the faithful, feed them, give them strength for spiritual struggle.'"[347]

III. Heroes of a great spiritual warfare

"Ars is no longer Ars!" Jean-Marie Vianney realized this one day, but he had not imagined that the conversion of his poor people would attract crowds and therefore extend his spiritual struggle beyond all borders. His reputation as a confessor became legendary, forcing him to hold endless sessions in the confessional, his privileged place of penance and mercy. "We offend the good Lord so much that we would be tempted to ask for the end of the world! ... We must come to Ars to know what sin is.... We only know what to do there: we can only cry and pray." The saint forgot to add that

[347] Benedict XVI, General Audience, Wednesday, August 5, 2009; cf. *Presbyterorum Ordinis*, no. 6.

he was also taking part in the atonement: He confided to those who asked his advice, "I give them a little penance and do the rest in their place."[348]

Faced with the sinner's obstinacy and ingratitude towards such a good God, tears sprang from his eyes: "Oh, my friend," he said, "I cry because you do not cry!" But with what delicacy and fervor did he not revive hope in repentant hearts. Untiringly, he made himself among them the minister of divine mercy, which was, he said, powerful, "like an overflowing stream that drags hearts in its path," and more eager than a mother's solicitude, for God is "more ready to forgive than a mother would be to pull her child from the fire."[349]

This intimate struggle of mercy with sinners from heart to heart is accompanied by a hand-to-hand struggle with the Enemy of human nature, the Evil One, whom he almost familiarly called "the Grappin." To his attacks of all kinds, aggressive and repeated, to hinder his ministry, the holy priest benefited at the beginning from the support of some parishioners who noticed, helplessly, the strangeness of the phenomena. Noises, fires, jostling, waking up, cold anguish: everything goes from the myriad of diabolic manifestations that the wrestler learns to interpret and circumvent for the benefit of his apostolate.

Although harassed by the Grappin, the holy priest was nevertheless fighting another battle against himself, by the mortifications we have mentioned, which were added to the vigorous asceticism of the evangelical counsels of poverty, chastity, and obedience. What a splendor, its purity and obedience! Moreover, he accepted without complaint the crosses inherent in his ministry: "Slanders

---

[348]*Vatican Secret Archives*, vol. 227, p. 1018, quoted in Saint John XXIII, *Sacerdotii Nostri Primordia*, n. 83.

[349]Saint John XXIII, *Sacerdotii Nostri Primordia*, nn. 86, 87, 88.

of people, misunderstandings of a vicar or confreres, contradictions, and also a mysterious struggle against the infernal powers, and sometimes even the temptation of despair within a spiritual night."[350] Saint John Paul II concluded his letter to priests on Holy Thursday 1986 by affirming "that the figure of the Curé d'Ars does not pass" and that, consequently, participation in the cross of Christ expresses the identity of the priest, his union with the Love of the Heart of Jesus for sinners: "In the priest, Christ lives again his Passion for souls. Let us give thanks to God who thus allows us to participate in the Redemption, in our hearts and in our flesh."[351]

Finally, the spiritual struggle of the Curé d'Ars has a much broader and more significant dimension that Benedict XVI has highlighted:

> Far from reducing the figure of Saint John Mary Vianney to an example albeit an admirable one of eighteenth-century devotional spirituality, on the contrary one should understand the prophetic power that marked his human and priestly personality that is extremely timely. In post-revolutionary France which was experiencing a sort of "dictatorship of rationalism" that aimed at obliterating from society the very existence of priests and of the Church, he lived first in the years of his youth a heroic secrecy, walking kilometers at night to attend Holy Mass. Then later as a priest Vianney distinguished himself by an unusual and fruitful pastoral creativity, geared to showing that the then-prevalent rationalism was in fact far from satisfying authentic human needs, hence definitively unliveable.[352]

[350] Saint John Paul II, Letter to Priests for Holy Thursday 1986.
[351] Ibid.
[352] Benedict XVI, General Audience, Wednesday, August 5, 2009.

Jean-Marie Vianney's great spiritual warfare, spread over a lifetime, thus has a prophetic value for the new evangelization, because it teaches to sow joy in consciences and communities, unlike the bitter and desolate fruits of a humanism without God.

I would be remiss if I did not finally mention the greatest secret, perhaps, of this holy priest freely chosen by God to save the sinners of a proud and tumultuous time. The biographers of the Curé d'Ars do not fail to note a small family incident that occurred one evening in the sad year 1789. Jean-Marie is a little over three years old, and he has disappeared. His mother is looking for him, anxious, fearing that he has fallen into a small pond where the animals drink. As she walks past the stable, she hears the whispering of a childish voice. She enters without noise and discovers Jean-Marie, kneeling on a layer of straw, very close to the gray donkey and the sheep, mumbling prayers while staring in amazement at a small statue of the Virgin Mary he holds in his hands. Mrs. Vianney lifts him up and embraces him to her heart, gently reproaching him: "Why hide to pray? You know well that we pray together."

A small family scene revealing a love for the Virgin that preceded the child's subsequent knowledge of her.[353] "Has the Curé d'Ars seen the Most Blessed Virgin?" Bernard Nodet replied that "the number of testimonies according to which it seems that it was related to extraordinary facts, indicate that there is surely a background of truth there."[354]

In any case, the Curé d'Ars knows her intimately, and he sees the Blessed Virgin very close to the Blessed Trinity; he knows that she participates more than anyone in God's radiance: "As soon as she is created, the Blessed Virgin is full and walks in the great ocean of

---

[353] Françoise Bouchard, *Le Saint Curé d'Ars: Viscéralement prêtre*, 2nd ed. (Paris: Salvator, 2009), pp. 17ff.

[354] Nodet, *Vianney*, p. 26.

grace." "The heart of this good mother is only love and mercy. And since she only wants us to be happy, it is enough to turn to her to be fulfilled."[355] Finally, the holy priest, adorer of the Real Presence, joining his extraordinary Eucharistic devotion to his secret love of the Virgin Mary, recommends at the end this prayer, both Trinitarian and Marian: "A prayer very pleasing to God is to ask the Blessed Virgin to offer to the Eternal Father her Divine Son."[356]

Other words and anecdotes of the holy priest would be worthy of our attention and would nourish our devotion and esteem for the priesthood. There is no doubt that Jean-Marie Vianney lived with fear and trembling his vocation to the priesthood and his responsibility as a pastor. He was often tempted to flee from it to take refuge in penance and "mourn his poor life." But he held on with the help of his bishop and his parish community. His grandiose vision of the priesthood sustained his total and selfless consecration to the service of his sheep.

Nowadays, this vision is still valid, but it benefits from being integrated into the more complete sacramental ecclesiology of the Second Vatican Council. This integration, however, does not justify diluting the specificity of the vocation to the priesthood in an undifferentiated promotion of all vocations. Many young people feel sometimes deceived and do not respond to a discounted proposal of the greatness of the priesthood. What the Curé d'Ars experienced in his parish as pastoral charity, discernment of charisms, and Christian formation is a magnificent illustration of the wonderful correspondence between the hierarchical priesthood and the priesthood of the baptized, both participants in the one Love of the Heart of Jesus.

On the other hand, the asceticism of the holy priest frightens us, rightly so, and we applaud the idea that he is no longer

[355] Ibid., p. 27.
[356] Ibid.

imitable today in his materiality. But can priests do without authentic asceticism of heart, body, and spirit if they want to witness the pastoral conversion required for our time? In this regard, Pope Francis provides us with strong guidelines that broaden the ascetical perspective of pastoral service in a communitarian and missionary sense. Many of his exhortations promote the fight against spiritual worldliness, careerism, sterile pessimism, selfish acedia, division, hypocrisy, gossip, ambiguities, and double life sometimes hidden under pious appearances.[357]

Against these ecclesiastical vices, but not exclusively, we need a vigorous asceticism today as in the past—an asceticism conducted in the new context of networks and instruments of human communication with unprecedented development, and accompanied by the transmission of a "mystic" of living together in a positive and joyful way: "Authentic faith in the Son of God made flesh," concludes Pope Francis, "is inseparable from self-giving, community belonging, service, reconciliation with the flesh of others. In his Incarnation, the Son of God invited us to the revolution of tenderness."[358]

Conclusion

At the end of this brief mention of some of the virtues, words, and gestures of the holy Curé d'Ars, I have no great new idea to offer for the pastoral and missionary conversion preached by Pope Francis. But I would like to see the conviction emerge that there is no ideology, no enthusiasm, no charism, no recipe that can make up for the holiness of priests that generates the holiness of the faithful.

Through the gift of the holy Curé d'Ars, God converted His people once and for all, and He showed once and for all how we can always promote the pastoral conversion of our communities:

[357] *EG*, nos. 76-109.
[358] *EG*, no. 88.

Friends of the Bridegroom

Prayer, penance, charity, preaching, and poverty are the resources of the Gospel from the beginning. It is up to all of us priests, lay and religious, to draw abundantly from it the Love of the Heart of Jesus, which plunges priests and Christian communities into the Eucharistic and Marian source of Trinitarian communion. Like an ever-growing living water, this infinite source flows through us for our joy and to quench the thirst for a disoriented world, thirsty as we are for the promises of eternal life.

At a time of new challenges posed by the increasing globalization of indifference and individualism at the expense of solidarity and peace among peoples, we really need a new evangelization where "the proclamation focuses on the essential, on what is more beautiful, greater, more attractive and at the same time more necessary."[359] This is why the virtuous figure of the holy Curé d'Ars—his message of mercy, the fruitfulness of his priesthood in the priesthood of his parishioners, his powerful intercession as patron saint of the priests of the whole world, his whole evangelical life full of meaning for all times—ultimately gives us nothing less than the risen Christ, the only Savior of humanity. The parish of Ars and the universal Church have no other message than this hope.

* * *

"Take my yoke upon yourself" (Father Olier)[360]

Come to me.... Take my yoke ... and you will find rest.[361]

Dear brothers and friends,

These words of the Gospel, which the liturgy of the day offers, seem to me to be rich in meaning for a fraternal encounter that is

[359]EG, no. 35.
[360]Grand Séminaire de Montréal, July 17, 2003.
[361]Mt 11:28-29.

part of the profound renewal taking place in Saint Sulpice. I am particularly happy to be in your midst in this chapel of the Major Seminary, carrying a new pastoral mission that I have come to entrust to your fervent prayers. Thank you for having had the idea of this fraternal reunion after all the happy and moving adventures of recent years. Let us rejoice in the spirit of our masters and founders who watch over us from Heaven.

"Come to me, all you who labor and are burdened, and I will give you rest." To go to Jesus Christ, to become His disciples, to learn to know Him, to love Him and to serve Him, keeping Him carefully before our eyes, in our hearts, and even in our hands: Is that not all we have learned from Jean-Jacques Olier? Is it not this school of communion with the virtues and mysteries of the incarnate Word, through the power of His Spirit, that has fascinated us and linked us to the French School and Saint Sulpice?

"Take *my* yoke upon you, and you will find rest." These words bring us particular consolation at this time, for the fatigue of the ministry, the aging, and the questioning of our time involve trials and pains that make us long for the rest of which the Lord speaks. Note, however, that Jesus does not say: "Take your yoke as I took mine"; He says: "Take *my* yoke upon you." What does He mean by *His* yoke? Would it be to become His disciple, to go to His school and find comfort and rest in His gentle and humble Heart? No doubt, but Father Olier can take us further in the interpretation. How did he himself carry this yoke of Jesus?

The parish of Saint Sulpice was the worst known area in Paris. Violent resistance hailed the beginnings of Father Olier's preaching and reforms. But, by the power of the Spirit, he was able to transform the environment, restore the spiritual dignity of the priests, and begin the work of the seminaries. All this in a few years, with intense contemplation and a very active apostolate. How did he do it? The answer is simple: he had taken *Jesus'* yoke upon himself and found it light, because of the bond that united him to his Master, because of the Spirit. To take upon oneself the yoke of Jesus and leave oneself to the Spirit is the same thing. It is the surrender to grace.

Jean-Jacques Olier had understood at the end of a heavy trial that it was necessary to renounce building the house himself, that he had to leave himself to the Spirit and abandon himself to divine mercy, passing through the annihilation of the sinful self, stuck in the cloak of self-love, pride, and envy. He had understood the call of the Burning Bush to forget himself in adoration, to let himself be burned in a fire of Love that consumes without destroying, and to bear the Name of the Savior God to a people reduced to slavery.

We are the heirs of this priest, who renounced the episcopate three times in order to devote himself better to the evangelization of peoples through the sanctification of the clergy. He embraced that yoke of his Master, which seemed light to him because of the Gospel of the Spirit, that mysterious Trinitarian bond that makes all the disciples one with Jesus, the Son of the Father. It is indeed the "magic" of the Holy Spirit to make one what is multiple, to make ours what is His, in all truth, by putting His preaching in our mouths to generate divine life in souls, by pronouncing His words that give His Body to eat and His Blood to drink, for the joy of faith. Is not this good news of the Spirit our secret to face serenely the fatigue, failure, and cultural collapse of Christianity, of which we are helpless witnesses?

At the school of Jean-Jacques Olier, we learn to bear this soft yoke of the Spirit in the manner of the beloved disciple, who took Mary into his home and learned from her the gentleness, humility, and light running of her charity in bearing the Son of the Most High and the joy of the Spirit to the great family of the children of God. Saint Sulpice lives on this heritage, which has preserved its missionary spirit, its somewhat controversial reputation, and its message of hope, which is penetrating new environments, even in this country.

May the devotion to the Holy Family and the corresponding ecclesiology, which deeply inspired the founders of the Canadian Church, renew us in hope, following in the footsteps of the gentle and humble Master of hearts, Whose holy name we bear three times in our hearts and in our hands. May the grace of the Spirit, like a great river of life, unite Sainte Anne de Beaupré and Saint Joseph du Mont-Royal with the Luminous Rosary that links Notre Dame du Cap with Notre Dame de Québec and Notre Dame de Montréal. May the Spirit of Saint Sulpice, who has never ceased since the beginning to spread contemplation within the priesthood, bring forth new priestly vocations on the fertile humus of the Christian family, renewed in the image of the Holy Family of the incarnate Word.

Duc in altum. Nothing is lost as long as faith lasts! "Come to me, take my yoke upon you, and you will find rest."

Chapter 8

The Priest, a Given Man

The debt of mutual love[362]

Owe nothing to anyone, except to love one another, for the one who loves another has fulfilled the law.[363]

Dear friends,

This Sunday's liturgy reminds us that the perfect fulfillment of the Law is love. The Apostle Paul speaks not only of love in general, but of mutual love. The Gospel tells us the concrete demands of this love in the lives of Jesus' disciples—requirements that are particularly relevant in a training environment such as the Major Seminary.

Do not keep any debt except the debt of mutual love. First of all, he talks about debt, because, as far as love is concerned, we are indebted forever, and we will remain in deficit all our lives. This word of the Apostle goes beyond a pious exhortation; it underlines a fundamental fact: We really have a debt of love towards each other that we must not forget. Where does it come from, and what does it commit us to?

---

[362] Major Seminary of Montreal, homily to seminarians.
[363] Rom 13:8.

Friends of the Bridegroom

Before we look at the implications, let us look at the rationale. This foundation is not the bond of flesh and blood, nor the belonging to the same group for the same ideal. This foundation is Jesus Christ, the love of Jesus Christ, Who, at the cost of His blood, reconciled us to God and to each other. Christ took our sins upon Himself, out of love, and destroyed the wall of hatred that separates humans from God and their fellow human beings. This redemptive love has made us members of His Body, animated by the same Spirit and responsible for the same witness, each according to his own vocation.

This love seized us at Baptism and marked us with a seal that indicates our belonging to Christ through our living bond to the Church. The love lived and witnessed by Christian communities illustrates the Sacrament of Baptism, which makes us live the life of the risen Christ. "It is by this sign that you will be known for my disciples, by this love that you will have for one another."

Dear friends of the Major Seminary, dear seminarians, and dear formation team, this word comes at the right time for a new school year and for the Rite of Admission to Candidacy for Ordination as Deacons and Priests. It places us before the essential: mutual love rooted in the love of Christ. The challenge of training is to learn this to the point of being living examples and credible messengers.

In Cologne, the Holy Father Benedict XVI reminded seminarians all over the world that the seminary is "less a place than a significant time in the life of a disciple of Jesus."[364] It is a time of demanding study but, above all, a time of discovery of Christ, a time of growth in His intimacy.

I personally have a good memory of my time in the seminary, despite the upheavals that the local Church experienced during

---

[364] Benedict XVI, Apostolic journey to Cologne on the occasion of the 20th World Youth Day, Meeting with the seminarians, August 19, 2005.

my formation. It was a time of experience of God and fraternity, a learning of mutual love. I remember in particular some of the experiences of life review that we had as a team, where we tried to practice the fraternal correction that the Gospel recommends today.

The mutual love that we are called to live in the seminary cannot be limited to tolerance, respect for each personality, encouragement, and mutual aid; it must reach the level of a humble and delicate correction of one another. This is not easy, but it is possible in a spirit of humility and prayer.

The life of the seminary is not only a time of residence together during studies. It is a laboratory of the Gospel, a school of communion, where everyone must expect to be accompanied and corrected, in order to acquire the priestly formation desired and proposed by the Church. The formation team obviously has a central role to play in this regard with the loyal and eager collaboration of everyone.

One does not become a priest overnight, nor without an experience of spiritual deepening and apostolic availability. To become one of those "watchers" of which the prophet Ezekiel speaks, who are able to announce the Word of God and warn the lost, requires personal and community training and asceticism. Growth in love and service is at this price.

I encourage you to read and reread the dense and beautiful messages of Pope Benedict, who is winning more and more hearts and minds with his humility and authenticity. In his message to the seminarians, he invites us to the true adoration of Jesus in the house of the Church, which is symbolized by the manger in Bethlehem. It is in the Church that we discover Jesus with Mary, His Mother, who teaches us to love and follow Him.

Let us unite today in prayer to thank God for gathering us here for this time of formation. Let us be grateful for those who commit themselves to the Rite of Candidacy, thus marking their firm will to follow Christ on the path of the priesthood.

May our prayer be broadened to the dimensions of the world, and may it become intense for the future of our Church, and especially for the increase in priestly and religious vocations. The awakening of the mission of the laity does not reduce the need for priests; on the contrary, it increases it and makes it more urgent. May the Lord bless us with new vocations like those that come to us and make us happy this year.

I wish you a fruitful and rich year of experiences of God and fraternal life. Take good advantage, dear seminarians, of your time of formation to discover your debt of love for Christ and your call to witness to mutual love among yourselves and with those who will be entrusted to you.

May this Eucharist help us to become aware of our belonging to the Mystery of the Body and Blood of Christ, which is the daily nourishment of our enthusiasm and our witness of mutual love. Amen!

* * *

"Do not be afraid"[365]

Jesus said to Simon, "Do not be afraid, from now on you will be catching men." When they brought their boats to the shore, they left everything and followed him.[366]

Dear friends,

We are all concerned about the event that brings us together today at the cathedral. The ordination of a priest is a miraculous

[365] Basilica Cathedral of Quebec City, ordination homily, February 7, 2010.
[366] Lk 5:10-11.

catch of fish. A priest is a multiplier. Let us think of all the people a priest meets and accompanies in his life with the Word of God and the sacraments. It is a miraculous catch, because a priest does more than give a fish to someone who is hungry, or teach fishing to someone who has to support himself. The priest is a community leader and a spiritual father. He is called upon to fish with others, so he is called upon to practice community fishing, industrial fishing, one might say. It is a multiplied fishing, because it is not only priests who are fishers of men. All the baptized open to the Spirit receive a charism, a personal gift to share with others. In forming a community, the priest constitutes this network of faith, love, and hope that makes all those who receive the Word of God, and who receive the sacraments — in particular the Eucharist — fall into the arms of God.

This appeal is addressed today to A., our brother. I heard this call again with a group of priests from Quebec City last October on Lake Tiberias. We were on a pilgrimage, and, in a boat, we meditated on the story of the calmed storm. When we returned from this pilgrimage, we felt with new strength this desire of the Lord: From now on, you will catch men. Not dead fish, but men, whom you will make more alive through the Word of God and the sacraments. Saint John XXIII used to repeat that the priest is the fountain of the village. In small Italian villages, people used to come to the fountain to draw water and bring it home, and thus water and feed the family. The priest is the fountain of the village, where people run for advice, a kind word, a word of consolation and reconciliation, for the forgiveness of which Saint Paul speaks in his letter today. This is the ministry of reconciliation and peace that the priest is called to exercise so that the baptized may be more radiant with God's grace, and so that communities may be more attractive to all.

The holy Curé d'Ars, whom we mention especially in this Year for Priests, began in his very small village with a conquering charity and the strength of prayer. He was interested in farmers; he asked them about their difficulties. He listened to his parishioners and saw their needs. Of course, he shut down the cabarets that were the cause of Ars' misery. But he took care of the fiddler and the little girls who worked in these cabarets. He helped them with charity, and some of them even became fervent apostles in the parish. The holy priest was a man of the people, a man of fervent prayer and Eucharistic adoration. We know how much he was the man of reconciliation and forgiveness with his twelve to fifteen hours of presence in the confessional, winter and summer. But the Curé d'Ars conquered his parish through his prayer, his charity, his humble word, and his perseverance. We invoke it on this day, in this ordination that brings us together.

Dear A., here you are on the shore, in response to the call of the Lord. Your answer challenges us all. We see that you are ready to leave everything to follow the Lord, to be with Him in this ministry of life, reconciliation, and love. He invites you to leave everything. You have already left your family ties, and your mother's departure is still very recent. She, who carried your vocation in her prayer and suffering, is certainly with us on this feast day, in this jubilation that dwells in us today, in this thanksgiving. I tell you to count on grace. Jesus calls, and Jesus enables us to be faithful, to carry His Word and to be carried by His Word. For it is the Word of Christ that carries you, much more than you do the Word. This Word that we repeat in every Eucharist for the people of God: This is my Body, delivered for you; this is my Blood, shed for you. This word is pronounced by Christ, and you simply give Him your mouth, your spirit, your faculties so that this word may continue to produce its effect, to give us the Body of Christ and His Precious Blood as heavenly food. These goods that the world cannot appreciate, but that we know only by faith, and that we repeat each day or each week — each Sunday these words of Love that make us one with Christ.

Dear A., trust, have no fear. The Lord asks you to leave everything. He will give you back a hundredfold family and friends. You already have this welcome in the Family of Emmanuel, this new community full of life, of missionary enthusiasm that comes to us now to help us in evangelization. I am happy to greet this community and all their friends. I wish you happiness as a priest in this community, in the presbytery of Quebec City, and in the heart of the people of God as a spiritual father, a leader of this people, a multiplier of vocations.

Dear brothers and sisters, we are all uplifted by this event. First of all, in thanksgiving. Let us thank God for giving us a priest today, let us thank Him from the bottom of our hearts. All of us are already receiving new life from this event, a new impetus, a personal grace. May this grace give us the desire to be holier, to be more faithful to the will of God in our lives, to be spouses, consecrated in religious life, laypeople in whatever field. All of us are called to holiness, to the fulfilment of God's will through the perfection of charity. We are challenged to ask for new vocations to the priesthood and consecrated life — these vocations that we need so much in our country, in the province of Quebec, in our archdiocese. Today, we are asking for new vocations, holy vocations. Let us follow up this miraculous fishing together. Amen!

* * *

**"This is my command: Love
one another as I have loved you."**[367]

Dear friends and confreres in the priesthood,

I am happy to celebrate with you, the day after the canonization of seven new saints, this Mass of Thanksgiving on the occasion

[367]Homily for the 150th anniversary of the Apostolic Union of the Clergy, October 22, 2012.

of the 150th anniversary of the Apostolic Union of the Clergy. I thank Monsignor Julio Daniel Botia, your president, for his kind invitation, and I cordially greet the members of the executive board, each of you here present, as well as, through you, all the members of your association.

In a world subject to so many changes, it seems significant to me to highlight 150 years of existence. Born in 1862, under the auspices of the Séminaire des Missions Étrangères de Paris, the Apostolic Union of the Clergy has been maintained over time and has spread throughout the world; I note that it is now present in more than seventy-two countries and has thirty-five thousand members, which is impressive. God be blessed and thanked for this fruitfulness.

The Apostolic Union of the Clergy invites each of its members to grow in order to increase the *quality* and *quantity* of diocesan clergy in each diocese. This objective seems to me to be of particular importance in the current context. We are all suffering from the crisis affecting the clergy. Membership has declined, but not everywhere in the world; scandals have broken out, and the temptation to be discouraged can sometimes weaken apostolic zeal. The growth in number and quality that you are promoting in such circumstances represents a formidable challenge that brings us back to the essence of the Gospel.

"This is my commandment: love one another as I have loved you."[368] Jesus gives in testament to His disciples the commandment of mutual love. First of all, He enjoins them to love one another as He loves them, and He entrusts them with the responsibility of announcing this command.

At first glance, one would think that love cannot be ordered. Is it not in its nature to be free and gratuitous? Then why does the Lord make it such an insistent command? To understand it, we must

[368] Jn 15:12.

go back to the supreme source of Love: God. God is Love, absolute Love. Love is the only law governing the intimate relationships of the divine Persons.

Jesus introduces us into this Kingdom of Love, and He must enable us to participate in it. Jesus Himself is the gift of this Love, and He enables His friends not only to correspond to it but also to communicate it to all. Hence His command, which is at the basis of all Christian spirituality, especially that of priests. To enter the Kingdom of Love, Jesus therefore commands us to love Him with the same love with which He loves us, for we are His friends. In order to ensure this unity and reciprocity in love, Jesus commands His friends to love one another as He loves them, because, in fact, He gives what He commands. His commandment of love presupposes the gift of the Holy Spirit, Who pours Love into our hearts. There are therefore three fundamental reasons that justify Jesus' new commandment: the Kingdom as the goal to be achieved; Jesus' friendship, which requires reciprocity; and the gift of the Holy Spirit, which ensures unity in love.

To love God with all our hearts and to love one another with the same love with which God loves Himself: That is our vocation as Christians and priests. In this love poured into our hearts and freely embraced by us shines the glory of the Holy Trinity, which is absolute mutual Love, Three Persons, one Love. One God. The Fathers of the Church, especially Saint Augustine and Saint Gregory of Nazianzus, drew from this great mystery the inspiration for their thoughts and lives.

To priests, Love is shared as friends of Christ, friends whom He associates with His own mission. Hence the particular nature of their love, which differs from the filial love of the baptized, the conjugal love of spouses, and even the nuptial love of consecrated persons. The special love of priests somehow includes these characteristics of the baptized, but its special property is to be paternal.

Friends of the Bridegroom

Through their love, priests generate the life of God in souls and accompany its growth in the persons and communities whose pastoral care they receive.

Their love springs from the supreme source, the Father, through their identification with Christ the Priest, and it reaches the hearts of believers through the joint action of the Holy Spirit. Let us be sure that the source is abundant and flows within us, despite our limitations and sins. Through our consecration, God commits Himself to make our words and sacramental gestures fruitful for the benefit of His children. His paternal love, which passes through our pastoral charity, does not spread in a vacuum and without a precise plan. On the contrary, it is all oriented towards the building up of the Body of Christ in all humanity.

Dear friends, I repeat to you in the name of Jesus: "Love one another as I have loved you." This "as" is not only exemplary; it is participatory. He does not only order an imitation; He orders a participation that is an extension of Jesus' own love. Moreover, He orders the pouring into us from the fatherly source so that the world may believe and divine life may be given in abundance.

The Apostolic Union of the Clergy celebrates 150 years of existence. The current ministry has changed a lot compared with the Christian context of its origins. But it seems that the Holy Spirit has been able to preserve the essential part of your testimony of love, as you have undergone the transformations that have marked your association. Let us thank God for this grace of fidelity in the midst of the trials of the present time. And let us ask for the grace to grow in holiness in the same Spirit of Christ, Who inspires in us Trinitarian communion.

In this regard, let us listen to the Holy Father Benedict XVI's urgent invitation to reread the texts of the Second Vatican Ecumenical Council in order to find inspiration and momentum for the new evangelization. The Council was, in fact, before the word, the launching of the new evangelization of the contemporary world. For us priests, the beautiful Decree *Presbyterorum Ordinis* remains a sure reference, especially with regard to the unity of our spirituality around pastoral charity.

Our contribution to the new evangelization, in the spirit and letter of the Second Vatican Council, is through the "spirituality of communion" proposed by John Paul II at the dawn of the new millennium in *Novo Millennio Ineunte*. This spirituality is rooted in the living consciousness of participation in Trinitarian communion with all other members of God's people: to love God, to love every neighbor in God and with God, to let oneself be drawn by the Spirit of Christ into the abyss of paternal, filial, and fraternal Love, which constitutes the very bliss of the divine Persons. This is the banquet of the Kingdom, of which we already have a foretaste on earth.

Dear fellow priests, we are not only guests at this heavenly banquet. As friends of the Lord, we are hosts who welcome the guests and serve them the bread and wine of the Word and the Body and Blood of Christ. The Holy Anointing that dwells in us makes the faithful taste the wonderful offering of which we are the unworthy but dazzled depositaries.

Between us who serve the Word and the sacraments, and others who serve in all possible forms according to the gift of the Spirit bestowed on each one, there is a communion that transforms isolated individuals into living members of the same Body, the Body of Christ, towards which we all tend, as well as towards our Head, our Master and Lord, the Spouse of the Church. With Him we want to be one in love and service.

That is why our ministry received from the Lord commands us to command the faithful in our turn: "Love one another as I have loved you." For this reason, we are invested with an authority that is not ours but that of Christ Himself. And this authority comes from the Father, since Jesus commands us in the Name of the Father, of Whom we are icons with Him by virtue of our ordination.

In the midst of the changes in this world, let us not forget who we are, not civil servants or mercenaries, but fathers and pastors, who take care of God's children for the love of the Father and who want to spread with Him divine life in abundance. What a sublime mission this participation in the sovereign fruitfulness of the Eternal Father is!

Over the past 150 years, your association has grown and spread to almost every continent. Take advantage of this pause for prayer and reflection to return to the source of our priestly joy and pastoral spirituality. This spirituality of communion becomes exciting again in the light of the Trinitarian mystery in which we are participants as baptized Catholics, but also in a particular way as icons of the Father.

Pope Benedict XVI declared Saint John of Ávila, a diocesan priest, a Doctor of the Church. Through his life and wisdom, this great evangelizer was the inspiration and father of many saints, including Saint Ignatius of Loyola. In the sixteenth century, he devoted himself unstintingly to the new evangelization of a dechristianized region of Spain. May he become a leading figure in your association since the Church has discerned in him a sure and fruitful reference for the spirituality of priests.

Enthusiastically cultivate the spirituality of communion that inseparably unites the Most Holy Trinity and the Eucharist, two mysteries of communion that make them one, since Christ's supreme offering on the Cross expresses His love for the Father, and His Resurrection from the dead, by the power of the Holy Spirit, is the Father's response to this Love. We share in this love of the Father and the Son through the outpouring in our hearts of the Holy Spirit, the fruit of their mutual love, which intimately commands us to love as the only way to holiness.

Since we are friends of Jesus by virtue of His choice and grace, let us participate in His Trinitarian love joyfully and faithfully, and may our enthusiasm in following Him lead many priests and faithful to grow in number and holiness: "Love one another as I have loved you." Amen!

* * *

"People of priests, priests for the people"[369]

The liturgy of the day offers us the most appropriate priestly texts for the event that brings us together. On the one hand, the Letter to the Hebrews speaks of the New Covenant, based on the one sacrifice of Christ, offered once and for all; on the other hand, the Gospel of Mark shows us Jesus' confrontation with the kingdom of Satan and his power over demons, reminding us of the hard struggle to drive the holy Curé d'Ars out of his parish.

Our priestly identity comes from these texts; thank God for the opportunity to meditate on them together in a liturgical context where the divine Word acquires a singular performative virtue, because of its fulfillment in the Paschal Mystery we celebrate. May the Holy Spirit open our minds and hearts to this Word and make our whole being available to His light and grace.

Let us begin with the Gospel of Mark proclaiming: "It is the end of the kingdom of Satan," since the Kingdom of God breaks into the world in Jesus, casting out demons and solemnly warning those who refuse to see in it the sign of God's salvation.

Some scribes interpret His exorcisms as a satanic work, which He cannot let pass, because it is the height of lies. That is why He gives them one of the harshest warnings in the New Testament: "All will be forgiven to the children of men: their sins and the blasphemies they may have spoken. But if someone blasphemes

---

[369] Homily in Ars, January 23, 2017. See Heb 9:15, 24-28; Mk 3:22-30.

against the Holy Spirit, he will never have forgiveness. He is guilty of an eternal sin."

When the blindness of His opponents reaches the point of denying the evidence of daylight, generalities about mercy have no effect, and it is necessary to strike hard and precisely to pull these sinners out of their guilty blindness. In speaking of blasphemy against the Holy Spirit, Jesus refers here indirectly to eternal Hell, because such a closing mind leads to it, and He wants to prevent them so that doubt settles in their minds and makes them think about the consequences of their attitude. For he who treats Jesus as Beelzebub denies Christ, refusing the light of the Spirit that confirms to the listeners, through faith, that God's salvation is at work in the words and deeds of Jesus. Hence Jesus' peremptory and solemn warning, which is a grace for hardened hearts, because only the prospect of a final condemnation can call them into question. After such a warning, the scribes of all times need only behave themselves not to fall into eternal Hell, where guilty blindness leads and where no one but Christ can prevent them from falling.

Let us note in passing that our good Pope Francis, so inclined to the language of mercy, sometimes calls out harshly to certain scribes and Pharisees of our time who are not conscious of obstructing the Kingdom of God by their attitude. Let us pray for them and for the unity of the Church.

The Letter to the Hebrews presents us with the final act of Jesus' great battle against Satan, to which the Gospel testifies: Christ offered Himself in sacrifice, once and for all, to take away the sins of many, and to give the promised eternal inheritance to those who are called and who believe in Him. This is the summit of His priesthood, the Paschal Sacrifice of the New Covenant, which simultaneously founds the "people of priests and priests for this people," called together to be a Sacrament of Salvation for humanity.

"The priesthood is the Love of the Heart of Jesus," said the holy Curé d'Ars. It is a love that descends from Heaven to enter the prison of each sinner, to loosen him from his chains, to pull him out of his darkness and finally expose him to the light of grace; a love that transforms the sinner from within and enables him to ascend to the Father with Jesus in an embrace of forgiveness and reconciliation.

Thus, the priesthood of the Heart of Jesus, a descending and ascending, paternal and filial priesthood, gives the capacity, on the one hand, to be a mediator with Him in unity with all the holy people of God, a true priestly people, a Mediator of salvation for all humanity; on the other hand, some are chosen and placed at the head of this people in the name of Christ, in order to represent the Father with Him, as humble servants of the Word and the Sacraments of the New Covenant.

The Holy Sacrifice that we are now going to offer to the Father from the depths of the bridal union of Christ and the Church reminds us daily of who we are and what we must do at the service of this people of priests: enlighten them with the Word of God, nourish them with the Eucharist, guide them, and even correct them on occasion, so that God may reign in them through the love authentically lived and spread, and the hope thus offered concretely to a world in need of salvation.

Dear friends, bishops, priests, deacons, laity, and consecrated persons, celebrating together in Ars is always for me, and no doubt also for you, a reminder of the wonder of the priesthood. The holy Curé d'Ars, who supported a hard fight against Satan, distinguished himself not only, first of all, by his performance of heroic virtues, but also by his humble daily fight for the poor sinner clinging to the mantle of the Virgin Mary, who converted his parish and confessed France, by the invincible force of grace in his sovereign humility, nourished every day by the contemplation of the Holy Eucharist.

Friends of the Bridegroom

The holiness of the Curé d'Ars shines in his indomitable passion to convert his parish. Is this not the true holiness of the minister of Christ, sacrament of the merciful Father: sanctifying His children, activating their filial priesthood, loving them by giving them the happiness of the gift of carrying the Spirit?

Dear friends, let us ask for the grace of a priestly renewal for our time that involves "the priestly people as much as the priests for this people" and that allows the communion of Trinitarian Love that Jesus came to spread on earth like fire to show more clearly. Amen!

* * *

"Give them something to eat yourself"[370]

Ave verum corpus natum de Maria Virgine, / vere passum, immo-latum in cruce pro homine: Hail, true body born of the Virgin Mary, who truly suffered and died on the cross for humanity.

Dear brothers and sisters, allow me to give my own testimony of faith in the Most Holy Eucharist in an outpouring of intimate joy, in union with your faith and to confirm it.... Here lies the treasure of the Church, the heart of the world, the pledge of the term to which every man aspires, even unconsciously.... Allow me to repeat to Christ, in the name of the whole Church, in the name of each one of you: "Lord, to whom shall we go? You have the words of eternal life" (Jn 6:68).[371]

Our good old Pope, who thus confesses his faith in the Holy Eucharist, has just proclaimed 2004-2005, the International Eucharistic Year. From the International Eucharistic Congress in October

[370] Homily for Corpus Christi, Quebec City, 2004.
[371] Saint John Paul II, Encyclical *Ecclesia de Eucharistia*, no. 59.

2004 in Guadalajara, Mexico, to the Roman Synod of Bishops in October 2005, the whole Church is invited to refocus Her attention on the mystery of the Eucharist, Her true treasure, which She knows to be the heart of the world and the hidden magnet of all the aspirations of the human heart. I am happy to echo today this call of the Holy Father, in our Cathedral of Notre-Dame de Québec and in the presence of several members of the numerous delegation that will represent our archdiocese in Guadalajara next October.

The feast of Corpus Christi, which we solemnly celebrate today, commemorates the Body and Blood of Christ, in accordance with the order of Jesus received at the Last Supper: "Do this in memory of me." The Church continues the sacrificial offering of Her founder, sacramentally, that is, under the veil of liturgical rites, but in all truth, because of the words of the Lord Jesus, which effect what they mean. "Take and eat," said Jesus on the night He was betrayed, "this is my Body, which is for you; this cup is the New Covenant in my Blood. Every time you drink it, do it in memory of me."[372] These words, spoken by the ministers of Christ, bring about what they mean because they are divine words whose effectiveness rests on the very authority of this divine Word.

One day, when a catechist was struggling to explain how it is possible for bread to become the Body of Christ and wine to become the true Blood of Christ, an eight-year-old child who was listening to him, suddenly inspired as children can be, raised his hand and said to him: "Jesus says it, He does it." "Jesus says it, He does it": What a wonderful truth! When Jesus speaks, the Word of God fulfills what it says. And to illustrate it, the Gospel reports the miracle of the multiplication of bread. A large crowd gathered around Jesus to listen to His Word, and the disciples were worried about the sunset and people's hunger. "Give them something to

[372] 1 Cor 11:25.

221

eat yourself," Jesus replied.[373] And, with the five loaves of bread and two fish, He distributes food for all these people. Everyone ate their fill, and twelve baskets of leftover pieces were picked up.

This gesture is symbolic. It prefigures the other gesture we have just recalled, that of the Eucharistic gift of His Body and Blood. The Church knows from experience the truth and realism of this gift. The Eucharist is more than a symbol; it is the reality of the Body and Blood of Christ, a supersubstantial food of which the material abundance of multiplied bread is the symbol. Yes, brothers and sisters, let us not hesitate to confess our faith in this wonderful gift, which calls for our adoration and our immense gratitude. How many benefits are given to us by this mystery! What an incomparable benefit spiritual and sacramental communion brings to this Mystery! There would be no consecrated life in the Church without this Mystery. The Church Herself would eventually disappear without this sacrament, because the Church lives on the Eucharist.

By giving us this consecrated bread and wine, Jesus gives Himself to us in His Body and Blood; we can thus assimilate it physically, but it is He who, in fact, assimilates us spiritually. By consuming the Body of Christ, we become spiritually members of His Body, which is the Church. "Receive what you are, the Body of Christ," Saint Augustine repeated to the Christians of Hippo. You commune with the sacramental Body, with His physical Body under the appearance of bread, and you become His Mystical Body, His ecclesial Body; you become what you are: members of His Body, who continue to give it hands to heal, feet to walk, tongues to speak, and hearts to love.

It must be recognized that many of the faithful, especially among the younger generations, have lost or never discovered the richness and beauty of this treasure. Let us not blame them, but let

[373]Lk 9:13.

us ask ourselves how we can help them to discover it. Let us take advantage of the Eucharistic year that John Paul II has just decreed to announce this good news of the Eucharist and to bear a more faithful witness to our faith in this Mystery. "Give them something to eat yourself," Jesus tells us again. Give food to all those around you who are hungry for bread and for the Word of God. Feed all those who suffer from hunger for friendship, hunger for respect, reconciliation, and peace. May our witness enlighten them; may our charity comfort them; may our friendship nourish them, and may it help them to discover the treasure of the Word of God and Sunday Mass. Under the cover of the humble Eucharistic rites, the risen Christ offers us a renewed hope and His incomparable friendship.

Yes, brothers and sisters, allow me to repeat to you, too, with John Paul II, my faith in this mystery, which is truly the treasure of the Church, the heart of the world, and the pledge of the Kingdom to come; this Kingdom is already bursting into our midst, at this Eucharistic table where the bread of the angels is shared with us. Amen!

Chapter 9

"Duc in Altum!"

Year of Mercy, Jubilee of Priests, priestly retreat guided by Pope Francis[374]

Dearest friends,

We are particularly blessed today to live this priestly retreat in the company of the Holy Father, animated by his witness and his word, happy to become more deeply aware of our vocation to Love, in the service of the Word of God.

On the eve of the solemnity of the Sacred Heart and in the context of the Jubilee of Mercy, we again feel great gratitude for the friendship of Christ Jesus, Who chose us "to be with Him" and to announce His word to our brothers and sisters. Looking back after ten, thirty, or fifty years of priesthood reminds us of many reasons for thanksgiving and praise to the merciful Lord. This look may also leave us with some reasons for sadness due to our faults and our poor response to the insignia of grace of our vocation.

This mixture of contrasting feelings should not surprise or disappoint us, however, because it stimulates us to renew our fundamental decisions, as Saint Ignatius of Loyola suggests in the

---

[374]June 2, 2016. See 2 Tim 3:8-15; Mk 12:28b-34; Ps 24.

Exercises, when he recommends to the retreatants to imagine the decision to be taken as we would like to see it again at the time of our death. In fact, all our life unfolds in the light of eternal life that illuminates and accompanies all our decisions. This retreat is a privileged opportunity to renew our unreserved yes to God, that is, a yes to the incomparable grace of our baptism, which flourishes in the yes of our response to the priestly vocation.

Today our poor, sinful weakness is especially taken care of and rescued by the divine mercy so widely offered and spread, which confers on the Eucharist that we celebrate a value of a renewed call to respond to the Love that becomes flesh through our hands, a call that lifts us up from our disappointments and carries us away in the Son's response of Love to His Father until death, a call that confirms the Spirit of holiness from which we have been anointed at our ordination by the imposition of hands.

Dear confreres in the priesthood, "remember Jesus Christ, risen from the dead." Remember His mercy towards you and His gratuitous friendship, which you joyfully show before men by freely giving His grace and His Word of truth. Remember Jesus Christ, Who places in your heart and on your lips His words of fire and blood, His ultimate words, spoken with His last breath, which contain Life more powerful than any death: "Your sins are forgiven"; these words of mercy that you have multiplied for your brothers and sisters with each absolution also contain for you each time a discreet, indirect, unheard-of grace, the grace to serve the passion of love of the Bridegroom that embraces each soul touched by this redemptive and re-creative Word.

This miraculous word, which no feat of this world can equal or surpass, does not leave the one who utters it unscathed by the wound it reveals, even if so many times you have uttered it out of duty and in a mediocre manner. His wound of love is always there, ready to heal you and sanctify you, provided that from time to time you let yourself be met and forgiven by this Word of resurrection and eternal life.

And what about this other eschatological Word that is entrusted to you to give life to the world, this Word that attracts everything in the axis of the Cross and the Resurrection, around which the cosmos and the history of nations revolves, this unique Word that confuses by its power and simplicity: "Do this in memory of me." Yes, do this, take the bread and wine, repeat the rite I have left you in the Testament, but do above all what it means of absolute Love for God and for all humanity.

"Listen, Israel: the Lord our God is the only Lord, and you will love the Lord your God with all your heart, with all your soul, with all your mind, and with all your strength. Here is the second one: you will love your neighbour as yourself." This first and second commandment have become one since Jesus united them inseparably in His life and crucified flesh. This new commandment of love is announced by us in word and deed, but it is, above all, effectively realized through the distribution of the Body and Blood of Christ, the supreme communication of the gift of His Heart. If our own testimonies of love always remain below the example of the Master, the sacramental gift that we celebrate and distribute to the faithful is always equal to the perfect unity of the two loves: that for the one God and that for all humanity redeemed by the Lord's Paschal Sacrifice.

Dear friends of the Bridegroom, remember the first embrace that seized you and delighted you to be friends of Christ and humble instruments of His grace; strengthened by His renewed friendship in this retreat, become ever more "sacrament" of His pastoral charity offered to all without distinction or restriction. Remember the look of the Bride, Who expects you to serve the Pastor and the Bridegroom in all purity and humility. Trust in the grace that dwells within you and frees you from yourself. Do not be afraid to love in complete freedom all the faithful entrusted to your care, in the Spirit of holiness that renews you every day at the Eucharist and that the Father of Mercy gives you abundantly again in this Jubilee Year.

With a deep sense of gratitude, let us now remember the Trinitarian Love that descends among us in the form of the sacrificed and victorious Lamb hidden under the sacramental signs; its unique glory dazzles our faith, covers our weakness, and fills us with intimate and radiant joy through communion. How can we respond to Him with anything but our readiness to bring to the world, serenely and joyfully, the wonders of mercy of the Father, through the Son, and in the Holy Spirit? May the grace and indulgence of the Jubilee consecrate us to it! Amen!

* * *

The Comforting Spirit comes![375]

There are hours in life when we priests and bishops need to be comforted. Let us humbly acknowledge that no matter how hard we face the challenges and keep calm in difficult times, there are disappointments and hours of weariness when our reserves of optimism run out and expose us to sadness and discouragement. We, too, like so many of our tried and tested followers, are forced to cry out to Heaven to be rescued and comforted. The experience of these painful hours can be very personal, or even communitarian, or even ecclesial in the universal sense.

I remember a very unexpected consolation that was given to me one day at the Marian shrine of my country, Our Lady of the Cape, after a difficult, if not stormy, episcopal meeting. I had entered the small chapel of the sanctuary to throw my sorrow into Mary's heart, and now, as I left the chapel, a young girl was waiting for

[375] Rome, Pilgrimage of the priests of Versailles, January 29, 2019.

me, in the rain; she was discerning a contemplative vocation and wanted to receive the blessing of her pastor before she entered the convent. Such examples have become very rare in Quebec, as you know, and all the more touching. I blessed this girl with all my heart, and our tears mixed with the rain without her knowing how much her gesture and prayer were an immense consolation to me. The Virgin Mary had quickly rescued me indeed.

Dear friends of Versailles, I welcome you to Rome with great joy the day after World Youth Day in Panama City—a colorful and warm celebration always full of hope and which has been a special grace for Latin America. I remember that in Paris in 1997, France contributed a lot to consecrating the WYD formula. I imagine that some of your priests have joined in this great event, which gives the world witness to the faith of young people and the concern of the Church, and of bishops in particular, for the evangelization of young people by young people.

Your pilgrimage to Rome is part of a time of trials that shake us up and humiliate us, not only at the level of our local Churches but also at the level of the universal Church. Let us look at the sad examples of last year, but let us not allow ourselves to be locked into a pessimistic attitude that forgets that in the midst of tribulations, the Holy Spirit also brings us consolation. The Holy Father exhorts us by his example and words to look to the future, where the Holy Spirit draws us to the Kingdom of God by offering us the consolation of His Presence among the holy people we serve.

On the plane to Panama, the Holy Father surprised me by giving me a copy of a book entitled *The Letters of Tribulation*. It is an update of a publication, made during his Jesuit provincialate, of the letters of Father Ricci, the Jesuit superior general in the years before the suppression of the Society of Jesus by Pope Clement XIV in 1774. Bergoglio then conveyed to his Jesuit companions how Father Ricci, in these very troubled times of persecution, did not lament or argue against the injustices suffered, but he invited his sons to return to the essentials, to intensify prayer and penance, to entrust themselves to the Virgin Mary and to welcome everything from the hands of God, in a spirit of humility, patience, and obedience. The reissue of these letters is paralleled by the letters that Pope Francis wrote to the people and bishops of Chile last year to help this Church overcome the crisis of sexual abuse. I assure you that this reading has done me great good and has helped me to understand the Pope's way of acting, his silence, his patience, and his trust in the Holy Spirit, Who guides God's people in history, amid human persecutions and divine consolations.

I am happy to welcome the initiative of your pilgrimage to Rome in these troubled times as a gesture of faith and openness to the newness of the Spirit. The initiative appears to me in itself to be a grace of the Spirit that opens you to other gifts. May you fully enjoy it in contact with the sacred places of our Catholic faith: the tombs of the Apostles Peter and Paul; the mother of all churches, Saint John Lateran; the first great Marian sanctuary of Christianity; and especially the meeting with the successor of Saint Peter, still blessed to be accompanied by his predecessor Pope Emeritus Benedict XVI. May all these places, symbols, and historical and living testimonies of the Spirit comfort you and animate you with a new hope.

You have expressed some expectations for me in relation to this conversation, while leaving me the freedom to share with you some snippets of my experience of ecclesial service. Allow me to remain in the register of consolation in a very broad sense, and to recall some facts of my experience as bishop, prefect of the Congregation of Bishops, and president of the Pontifical Commission for Latin America. Among the events that marked my episcopate in Canada, there was the International Eucharistic Congress in Quebec City in June 2008, which remains a pivotal date in my ecclesial experience. This event of the universal Church in a local Church made it possible to unite the living forces of the archdiocese around a service to the universal Church, which strengthened our sense of mission and ecclesial communion represented by the thousands of participants from the five continents. In addition to the spiritual, vocational and missionary repercussions of this event—the foundation of two seminaries, the setting up of an Internet broadcasting body, and financial support for a contemplative community—this event gave me the consolation of better understanding the mission of a particular Church. Indeed, the experience, lived with the help of parishes, the diocesan presbytery, and religious communities and movements, has created a new dynamic of communion and participation around the fundamental reality of Baptism, which Pope Francis strongly emphasizes in his letter to the undersigned concerning the mission of the laity in Latin America.[376] In this letter, the Pope condemns clericalism, which ignores Baptism and consequently gives rise to an erroneous, that is, dominant, exercise of the ordained ministry.

Although in different terms, I have long been affected by this same problem, and the experience of the follow-up to the 2008 Eucharistic Congress has opened me to a new theological and pastoral horizon. I then better understood the Trinitarian articulation of ecclesial communion, based on the Sacraments of Christian Initiation and the Sacrament of Orders, two complementary participations in the one priesthood of Christ. Since then, I have continued to deepen the relationship between the common priesthood of

[376] Pope Francis, *Les laïcs, messengers of the Gospel* (Paris: Salvator, 2016), pp. 14-15: "The first sacrament, which has forever sealed our identity and of which we should be proud forever, is baptism. Through him and the anointing of the Holy Spirit, the faithful are consecrated as a spiritual house, as a holy priesthood (*LG* 10)."

the baptized and the hierarchical priesthood of ordained ministers in the light of pneumatology. The gift of the Holy Spirit, Who constitutes the priesthood of the baptized is of a filial nature in accordance with the baptismal grace of divine sonship; the gift of the Holy Spirit, Who constitutes the hierarchical priesthood is of a paternal nature, in accordance with Christ's mission to represent the Father on earth: "Whoever sees me, sees the Father." These two participations in the one priesthood of Christ correspond and are supported by the grace of the Holy Spirit, Who unites them and strengthens their harmonious correspondence by the multiple and varied charisms that He adds freely and graciously, in order constantly to revitalize the communion of pastors and the faithful at the source of Baptism, solemnly professed in the various forms of consecrated life.

"Brothers, the gifts of grace are varied, but it is always the same Spirit. The functions in the Church are varied, but it is always the same Lord. The activities are varied, but it is everywhere the same God who acts in all."[377] In the light of this Pauline text, which affirms the action of the Triune God in the variety of ecclesial gifts, functions, and activities, I have better understood that the mission of the Church, the communion of the Church, is to serve the witness of the Trinity in history, a witness of communion where God expresses Himself, filially, through the baptized persons attentive to the Word and nourished by the Eucharist. God expresses Himself paternally through His ministers; God expresses Himself again, freely, in the freedom of the Spirit, through persons endowed with charisms at the service of communion and mission.

This Trinitarian witness of communion and mission is not only a "model" that we represent ourselves and that we would seek to implement as best we can. In fact, it is not we who are the protagonists

---

[377] 1 Cor 12:4-5.

as baptized, but God Himself, Who, by the grace of baptismal and ministerial consecration, becomes visible and active in the filial and fraternal life of the sons and daughters of God, in the participation in divine fatherhood of ordained ministers, as well as in the evangelizing fruitfulness of the communities of consecrated life and the movements of apostolates. In this pneumatological light, we better understand that the Church is the Sacrament of Salvation, since it is this people of God where the Communion of the divine Persons is expressed and shared in ecclesial relationships, between pastors and the faithful, between charismatic and hierarchical gifts, always pushing people and communities more towards communion and mission, in order to share the gifts received with all humanity according to God's plan in Christ.

During the presentation of the renewed diocesan organization chart, which illustrated in concentric circles the communion of parishes, based on the fundamental reality of Baptism, with communities of consecrated life, based on the solemn profession of Baptism, enriched by special gifts for community building and the proclamation of the Gospel, as well as with the community of deacons and presbyters around the Bishop in the Spirit of Service, a community of ordained ministers to support the exercise of the common priesthood of the baptized, I perceived more vividly than ever that the diocese was much more than an administrative unit with a chief town and parishes scattered throughout the territory.

A diocese is a sacramental unity, a communion of communities articulated from the sacraments that involve believers in the mystery of communion that is God Himself in His Trinitarian relationships. These relationships do not hover over the world in an inaccessible beyond; they are turned towards the world in an outpouring of graces and blessings whose concrete presence and salvific meaning in the sense of First Corinthians should be grasped more deeply: "Brothers, the gifts of grace are varied, but it is always the same Spirit. The functions in the Church are varied but it is always the same Lord. The activities are varied, but it is always the same God who acts in all."

All this may seem theoretical and abstract if we confine ourselves to words; in fact, it is a rather audacious sacramental vision that sees the unity of divine and human action, the unity of divine and ecclesial relations, in terms of participation and communion in the real and daily life of our communities.

This vision seems to me to be adequate to fundamentally counter the tendency towards clericalism, denounced by Pope Francis, where priests impose themselves unduly on laypeople according to their own ministry, ignoring the Spirit given to them to witness their baptism in the world within their specific human responsibilities. This theological vision makes it possible to think of clerical-lay relations in terms of theological communion and not in terms of the powers to be shared between them. Above all, it makes it possible to appreciate the filial dignity of the baptized and their authentic priesthood exercised by the theological virtues, thus preventing functional abuses that lead to a clericalization of the laity themselves, if they conceive their own vocation in terms of ecclesial apostolate, while their primary mission is to penetrate and permeate the temporal structures of the present world with the Spirit of the Gospel. "What would it mean for us pastors if the laity were to become involved in public life?" asks the Pope following the plenary session of the Pontifical Commission for Latin America. "This would mean seeking ways to encourage, support, and stimulate all the attempts, all the efforts already made today to keep hope and faith alive in a world full of contradictions, especially in favor of and with the poorest people."[378]

[378] Pope Francis, op. cit. p. 20: "Several times we have been tempted to think that the committed layperson is the one who works in

At the school of Pope Francis, a Jesuit with a Franciscan mysticism, one cannot remain passive in a quiet possession of the truth. For He who said "I am the Truth"[379] also said "I am the Way" to the fullness of Life. Hence His all-out relaunch of the mission to which the Apostolic Exhortation *Evangelii Gaudium* gives programmatic testimony. The Holy Spirit has therefore not finished surprising us and shaking us up, in the continuity of the great conciliar Pentecost whose consequences have yet to be measured, in terms of reform and missionary transformation of the Church. Hence Pope Francis's striking style, his freedom of speech and action, his prophetic language towards the great of this world, and his gestures of tenderness towards the little ones, the sick and the poor, as well as his language of mercy towards all, embodied in a culture of encounter without prejudice, and in the promotion of dialogue at all levels, be it in intra-ecclesial relations or in ecumenical or interreligious relations. The missionary Spirit of the Church works through dialogue and thus attracts the world to the home of the Trinitarian communion that inhabits the Church and gives Her Her sacramental radiance. The missionary Spirit of Pope Francis is therefore perfectly in line with the Trinitarian logic of the divine missions that are always "on the way out," leading the Church into a renewed impulse of charity towards all the poor and urging Her to proclaim at new costs a mercy without borders.

Returning to my own experience as president of the Pontifical Commission for Latin America, I would be remiss if I did not share with you the experience of the last Plenary of the Commission

---

the works of the Church and/or in the activities of the parish or diocese, and, rarely we have thought about how to accompany a baptized person in his daily life; how, in his daily work, with his responsibilities, he engages himself as a Christian in public life."

[379] Jn 14:6.

for Latin America (CAL), which Pope Francis asked us to devote to *women as a pillar of the building of society and the Church in Latin America*. Such a theme has forced us to increase our twenty members by about fifteen women, in order to conduct an informed reflection with the participation of representative and competent people.

This event was for me an opportunity to initiate a reflection for a theology of women, and especially to become aware of the responsibility of the Church in order to help women to realize their human vocation and ecclesial mission in all areas where their nature and charisms allow them to build human society and to embellish the Church as Body and Bride of Christ.

Meditating on the relationship between the Virgin Mary and the Holy Spirit then allowed me to deepen the nuptial mystery of God with humanity, and the involvement of the Holy Trinity in history from the relationships of the Holy Family of Nazareth, to the station of Mary at the foot of the Cross and at Pentecost. This is the way, in my opinion, to deploy the feminine genius in its own sense, which has yet to be explored in the light of the Virgin Mary, as Saint Edith Stein tried in our time, and not in the claim of the ordination of women which is a more insidious form of clericalism, as if the ministerial priesthood were a power and the only charism in the Church.

It seems to me more and more imperative that the promotion of women be assumed by the Church in a more determined and coherent way, in order to free them from the serious consequences of sin in their living conditions and their social and ecclesial status. Violence against women in a thousand ways since the original sin continues to offend God and humanity, depriving them of the precious resources of their human and spiritual fertility. This situation particularly affects Latin America, where the "macho" culture prevails, but the problem is universal in one way or another.

What a responsibility, moreover, to be acutely aware that universal access to higher education for women for nearly half a century cannot fail to bring about transformations in gender relations, in ways of conceiving family or social roles, in women's presence and cultural and political influence in public life. Are we not entitled to expect from this promotion of women a more humane, peaceful society that is more open to a civilization of love?

Finally, one last point before concluding these few reflections on the consolation of the Spirit in our time. In the midst of the difficult task of eliminating all forms of abuse that affect our ministry as priests and bishops, I also experienced the consolation of working to update the document *Mutuae Relationes* (Guidelines for Relations between Bishops and Religious in the Church, published in 1978), a document that was reworked at Pope Francis's request. It is a question of rethinking the recognition and integration of the charismatic dimension of the Church, and thus the personal contribution of the Holy Spirit to the communion and mission of the Church, both at the level of local Churches and of the universal Church. The document will discuss the co-essentiality of charismatic gifts and hierarchical gifts in the Church and will draw conclusions about the relationship between consecrated life, apostolic and ecclesial movements, priests and bishops.

This update is an important step in the reform of the Church driven by Francis, who himself comes from the charismatic realm of the Church, for a missionary transformation that does not respond to fashionable slogans, but to the sacramental nature of the Church, which the Second Vatican Council has given pride of place by highlighting the Gift of the Holy Spirit and its repercussions in all areas of the Church's life and mission. In this regard, I am pleased to think that the witness of consecrated life in all its forms is an expression of the freedom and gratuity of the Holy Spirit, Who rejuvenates and embellishes the Church with His gifts and charisms,[380] thus constantly revitalizing the common priesthood of the baptized, as well as the hierarchical priesthood of ministers ordained in the service of the mission.

By way of conclusion: Come, Holy Spirit, Comforter!

Dear friends, these few reflections only initiate a conversation with you on the *theme of the consolation of the Spirit*. This is revealed to us as an intimate and dynamic presence that animates our priestly existence. It keeps us as diocesan presbyterates in the unity of a paternal charism at the service of the people of God's children who nourish their growth in divine sonship at the source of the Word of God and the sacraments. The face-to-face encounter between the people and the pastors is part of the relationship between the Father and the Son that the Holy Spirit brings into our human and ecclesial relationships. The more communion grows between pastors and the faithful, between pastors and families, the more the Spirit makes divine Life flourish in souls, and thus lay witnesses committed to the world and charismatic vocations in the service of the evangelizing mission.

There is no deeper and lasting consolation for us priests or bishops than to give ourselves, body and goods, to the Spirit of Love and Truth, allowing ourselves to be expropriated and distributed as the Body of Christ that we consecrate and share to build our ecclesial body within the glorious *kenosis* of His immolated and conquering love. This love is poured into our hearts through the inebriating fluidity of the Spirit, Who wants not only to console us, but to transform us into comforts for all those who seek God.[381] Is this not the best way not to withdraw sadly into ourselves during the time of tribulation?

---

[380]*LG*, no. 4.
[381]2 Cor 1:3.

"Duc in Altum!"

Beyond a conception of the priesthood too long limited to the service of ordained ministers, we must broaden the perspective and think of the priestly mediation of the Church Herself, as the Trinitarian articulation of the common priesthood and the hierarchical priesthood converges towards the fulfillment of the Kingdom of God, that is, towards the outpouring of the Spirit upon the world. Thus, in the most intimate part of the sacramentality of the Church, the centrifugal force of absolute Love attracts the whole creation into the blessed spiral of Trinitarian relationships: paternity, filiation, fraternity, unity, fecundity, freedom! Superabundant divine Life gushing out of the Eucharistic mystery!

What more could be said about the Comforting Spirit, other than He consoles us in His very Person. He does not only give an intellectual light that illuminates the trials we are going through. He does not only give a passing sense of relief such as a gesture or word of compassion can do for us. He gives Himself to us, confirming our sacramental union with Christ the Bridegroom through our service of nuptial love to the Bride-Church, in whatever state of mind we may find ourselves. He is a Gift-communion of a divine and ecclesial nature that integrates us into our own place of service in God's plan, with the joy of sharing in and contributing to the definitive joy of the marriage of the Lamb. Dear friends, happy pilgrimage! *Duc in altum!*